Supporting young people in Europe
Volume 2

Lessons from the 'second seven'
Council of Europe international reviews
of national youth policy

Howard Williamson

Council of Europe Publishing

French edition:
Soutenir les jeunes en Europe – Tome 2

ISBN 978-92-871-6202-1

All correspondence relating to this publication or the reproduction or translation of all or part of the document should be addressed to:
Council of Europe

Directorate of Youth and Sport
European Youth Centre
30, rue Pierre de Coubertin
F-67075 Strasbourg Cedex
Tel: +33 (0) 3 88 41 23 00
Fax: +33 (0) 3 88 41 27 77
e-mail: youth@youth.coe.int
http://www.coe.int/youth

Cover: Graphic Design Workshop, Council of Europe
Photo cover: PhotoAlto

Council of Europe
F-67075 Strasbourg Cedex
http://book.coe.int

ISBN 978-92-871-6203-8
© Council of Europe, April 2008
Printed at the Council of Europe

Contents

Executive summary

This monograph has two purposes. The first is to develop the framework that was initially established through a grounded reading of the material from the first seven international reviews of national youth policy[1] conducted through the Council of Europe Youth Directorate between 1997 and 2001 (see Williamson 2002). This has involved a careful reading of the subsequent national and international reports produced between 2002 and 2006[2] to identify those issues that merit either greater prominence or their introduction for the first time. The outcome of this exercise is the proposal of a new framework within which European-level debates on the subject of 'youth policy' should be taking place. The second purpose is, through consulting with those who have been part of these more recent reviews, to refine further the process by which international reviews are carried out. Though the response to requests for reflection and commentary from all those who had taken part was rather disappointing, it was sufficiently consistent and persuasive to suggest that there is immediate action that can be taken to improve the experience of participating in review teams and, thereby, ultimately, the quality of the international reports. Finally, the benchmarks against which 'youth policy' is, and might be, considered are outlined, indicating the need for further and more penetrating debate on an issue that is recurrently discussed but rarely reaches any definitive conclusion.

Section 1: Building on the 2002 framework

The proposed new framework does not dismantle the one first put forward in 2002. That was 'built' empirically from the documentation of the first seven reviews (seven national reports and seven international reports). By and large, subsequent reviews confirm that framework as reasonably robust, though these reviews also indicate that it requires some revision and amendment. The amendments have been made in the following ways:

- some new themes and issues, not apparent or relatively invisible in the earlier reviews, have emerged and therefore been added;

---

1. The first seven reviews were of Finland, the Netherlands, Spain, Sweden, Romania, Estonia and Luxembourg.

2. When the second synthesis report was proposed, it was anticipated that seven further reviews would have been concluded. In the event, the international review of national youth policy in Hungary was delayed, though it is now expected to take place in 2007. Furthermore, the international review of national youth policy in Armenia has not been concluded, though there is both a draft national report and an international report, which have provided material for this report. Thus this report is a synthesis report of youth policy international reviews of six countries: Lithuania, Malta, Norway, Cyprus, Slovakia and Armenia.

- some themes and issues, of greater prominence in recent reviews than in earlier ones, now demand more weight and attention within a new framework;
- within themes and issues that were already prominent in the "old" framework, there are points of significance that now require inclusion or a stronger focus.

In relation to concepts of 'youth' and 'youth policy', a number of new issues arose. Academic work on youth transitions has moved on considerably since 2002. The international reviews need to reflect more deeply on the increasingly polarised life experiences of young people, the relationship between childhood, youth and family policy, and the capacity of countries under review to produce a 'youth sociology' in their national reports that captures the 'social condition' of their young people. In terms of youth policy, the international reviews need to focus more sharply on the duration of current national youth strategies, their evolution (where they have come from, and how quickly), and the extent to which they seek to strengthen tradition or orchestrate change.

Five issues surfaced on the question of structure and infrastructure supporting youth policy. First, whether or not there was a formal legislative basis for youth policy seemed to be less important than the political commitment to engaging with and advocating for youth policy through administrative arrangements. Second, the relationship(s) between youth NGOs and their governments, which can always be argued as both problematic and beneficial whatever their particular form, is worthy of greater scrutiny. Third, understanding precise absolute and relative funding allocations to youth policy remains a significant challenge. Fourth, where national youth agencies (not national agencies for the EU youth programmes, but arm's-length government agencies responsible for youth issues and youth affairs) are in place, their roles and responsibilities merit close attention. Finally, the increasing presence of children's Ombudspersons or Commissioners means that there should be independent support, advocacy and representation for young people up to the age of 18 (the definition of 'children' within the UN Convention on the Rights of the Child, to which virtually all countries in the world are now signatories); their role, resources and activities should be legitimate territory for the international reviews.

Though not a new issue, the more recent international reviews make it very clear that a central focus of the reviews should always be how the aspirations of the central administration are 'cascaded' to operational effect; in other words, what are the 'delivery relationships' that transform youth policy into practice?

Across a range of policy domains identified in the first proposed framework, the recent reviews broadly confirm their importance, though some additional themes do emerge. Within education, international reviews need to ensure a close focus on four matters: structure and organisation, curriculum content, delivery (pedagogical methods), and standards. Of particular relevance to wider youth policy considerations are two further issues: drop-out, inclusion and achievement in formal education, and the real understanding and practice of 'non-formal' education.

Once young people have moved beyond formal education, the prospect of training and employment has become increasingly blurred and blended with commitments in family life, leisure and learning – and, arguably, volunteering. Those excluded from the labour market may be engaged in the informal economy. Future international reviews will need to explore these complexities more carefully.

Health is also complex territory and it is important that the use of illegal drugs does not overwhelm the health agenda. Across the many health issues of relevance to youth policy (obesity, exercise, mental health, sexual health, and substance misuse), the key questions are not just about statistical evidence and prevalence but about health services and young people's awareness of and access to them.

It was very clear from the most recent reports that, on the matter of values and religion, the place of religion in the lives of young people has been hitherto somewhat underestimated and requires greater attention. In relation to leisure and culture, insufficient consideration has been given to the persistence of 'traditional' culture and leisure practices. Moreover, there are important questions concerning young people's access to leisure-time opportunities, and also the apparent decline of 'leisure' as young people dedicate more and more time to learning and the pursuit of qualifications.

The early international reviews questioned whether some issues in fact had any place in 'youth policy'. These included military service and family policy. It is important, therefore, to recognise that military service in some countries remains a powerful socialising agent of young people (usually young men). There needs to be attention both to the experience provided during service in the military, and to the nature and consequences of alternative service possibilities for young people. For different reasons, there also needs to be more focus on the role of families in the lives of young people – both their families of origin and their families of destination. The sustaining, and sometimes constraining, influence of families on young people means that family policy is already critically connected to youth policy and practice. This is also the case with housing policy, for access to affordable accommodation in the right places (significantly in places where young people wish to study) is a key element in debates about social inclusion and opportunity structures for young people. Housing was already a feature of the original framework but, as some of the early international reviews predicted, it is becoming an ever more central feature of youth policy deliberations.

Finally, in terms of thematic content, the recent reviews have pointed to the changing profile of youth crime which, arguably, both derives from and should contribute to the wider context of youth policy. Youth justice appears to be an often neglected youth policy domain, yet it relates significantly to young people who have succumbed most to disadvantage and risk in their particular societies.

While there were no new policy domains identified from the more recent reviews – just a re-balancing and re-shaping of existing domains – this was not the case with cross-cutting issues, where old issues attracted new strands and a number of new issues emerged.

Of the existing cross-cutting issues, youth participation and citizenship remains centre stage at least within the rhetoric; it will continue to be important for international teams to unravel its meaning in different countries and to document the repertoire of opportunities, experiences and initiatives that are considered to assist these outcomes. Similarly, reviews should interrogate public strategies established to promote social inclusion. On the topic of youth information the essential point that needs to be sustained is the nature of the services available and the ways in which they are (or are not) used by different groups of young people. These three 'cross-cutting issues' were, then, simply reinforced as central issues for the review process; they did not generate new themes.

New themes did, however, emerge in relation to multiculturalism and minorities. The recent reviews all had very different types of 'ethnic mix' and, together, they make it very clear that future reviews need to develop a far more calibrated and sophisticated perspective on the specific complexities of multiculturalism in particular countries. This will, however, require more engagement with less visible 'minority' groups, which has sometimes not taken place on international review visits in the past. There is a similar complexity with the issue of mobility and internationalism, which was initially conceptualised in terms of 'gap' years and the European YOUTH programme. It is, of course, more diverse than that, for both positive (education and employment) reasons and more negative (sex trafficking, hidden economy) reasons. Also in need of further unravelling is the question of equal opportunities, which is often addressed only in terms of gender and perhaps ethnicity and disability, rather than across a fuller spectrum to include sexual preferences and orientation.

New cross-cutting issues also emerged. Future reviews will establish how significant they continue to be, but evidence from the recent reviews suggests that they merit inclusion in a new youth policy framework. First, there is not only some question of the radicalisation of young people – new fundamentalist loyalties arising from the 'clash of civilisations' between the Christian and Islamic faiths – but also a more pressing question concerning reaction amongst young people – a resurgence of old racisms and extremisms, especially white supremacist neo-Nazi groups. Second, there is an emergent tension between global pressures and perspectives, and local traditions and expectations. This local-versus-global pressure can have particular effects on different groups of young people, propelling some towards the more reactionary tendencies indicated above. There are also the multiple and sometimes contradictory effects of new technologies, which remained largely unexplored in some of the earlier international reviews.

Within particular countries are key issues concerning the relationships between the centre and the periphery – and whether or not any 'regional' policy is in place attempting to bridge this gap. This links closely to the issue of urban–rural polarisation, as young people increasingly drift towards urban life for leisure, education and employment. International reviews need to explore whether this is simply accepted or whether there are policy measures to stem the tide and 'incentivise' young people to remain in, or return to, their home communities. There is also a question concerning the emergence of a youth policy 'elite', as youth policy actors reach a comfort zone – all those 'inside' may then consolidate their position at the expense of aspiring newcomers and outsiders.

Finally, there were two disparate cross-cutting issues. One was to do with the environment, suggesting that countries are now incorporating environmental awareness and responsibility into formal policy programmes (notably in schooling), rather than leaving the issue to NGOs and 'single issue' youth activism. The other – clearly reflecting the nature and history of some of the countries recently reviewed – was the role of diaspora in contributing in many different ways to the lives of 'its' young people.

The initial framework also suggested and discussed foundation stones for effective youth policy: the role of research, the training of professional practitioners, and the dissemination of good practice. These were largely confirmed by the more recent reviews, though they also produce the same critical questions about weaknesses in the relationships between research and policy, an absence of serious attention to training, and limited mechanisms for sharing and debating effective practice.

Section 2: The international review process — reflections and recommendations

Starting with the eighth review (of Lithuania) there has been a process for conducting the review, starting with a preliminary visit to establish a country's priorities. This informs the composition of the international review team (which has been put together by the Youth Directorate), one of whom is the designated rapporteur. Meanwhile, the country in question compiles its national report. There are then two visits, usually a few months apart. The rapporteur then produces a draft international report which is presented to a (public) national hearing in the capital city of the country concerned. Amendments are then made prior to finalising the international report in preparation for its publication. The two reports are presented formally at an international hearing with the Joint Council of the statutory organs of the Youth Directorate of the Council of Europe – the CDEJ (the intergovernmental steering group on youth) and the Advisory Council (composed of representatives of youth organisations in Europe).

That, at least, is the blueprint for the process. What follows below is both a set of developmental suggestions regarding the desired and intended process and a critique of the process as it has actually taken place on more than one occasion.

There was a view that the preliminary visit, which has to date always been conducted by the same individual, should involve other people from both within and beyond the Youth Directorate, so that they can 'learn the ropes'. There was general approval and support for the composition of the international review teams. However, it was suggested that there should be closer links to both the previous and the subsequent review – possibly through the involvement of a member of the previous team or the CDEJ member for the country just reviewed, and the involvement of a researcher from the next country to be reviewed (who might then lead on the production of its national report).

There has been considerable inconsistency in the content of national reports and it was felt that some stronger, firmer blueprint could now be suggested. Moreover, there was concern about the timing of national reports – some had not been made available until the international review process was well under way, and it was argued that there should be a more rigid adherence to the agreed process: in other words, the international team does not visit until the national report has been made available.

Although the composition of the international review teams was not an issue, there was concern expressed about the preparation of individual members, to ensure that they understood the process and their roles, and were supported in preparing themselves for participation in the process. There was also a more grounded issue to do with appropriate (i.e. full) reimbursement of the costs incurred by participants through their participation in the reviews.

Team relationships were almost universally applauded; where they were undermined was through misunderstandings and uncertainties about the division of labour within the team. Relationships were also put under some pressure because of the lack of time during many visits for members to explore with each other their sense of progress and direction, or even the primary conclusions of their work.

Hosting countries invariably extended magnificent hospitality to the international review team and organised a thorough programme of meetings and visits. However, sometimes the programme was completely overwhelmed with professional and social commitments, leaving no space for the international team to work on its own agenda. Such space needs to be asserted and defended in every visit. There also needed to be more clarity of understanding between international review team members about what needed to be done between the first and the second visit.

These questions about divisions of labour and roles and responsibilities spill over into the production of the international report. This has typically been left entirely to the rapporteur, though other members have sometimes undertaken to make a contribution (but rarely have they actually done so). And, like the national report, there is a strong case for establishing greater standardisation in the framework that should be adopted.

Most of the national and international hearings have gone largely to plan, but some have been imbalanced in the time available to different presenters, especially the rapporteur for the international report. As with other issues in the process, there needs to be a clear understanding (and enforcement if necessary) of the time allocations for different speakers and for comment and questions.

Finally, there has always been a question about follow-up to the international review process – and if so, when? Two years is often suggested, and the principle of follow-up is already established in CDEJ documentation on the review process. There is a powerful prima facie case, given the resources that have already been invested in a review, for ensuring that some 'follow-up' review also takes place.

There is little dissent about the value of the international youth policy review process. The proposals that have been advanced following a reflection on the current process are ideas that would ensure further improvement to a staged process that has, most admit, gone a little 'pear-shaped' in recent years. The format devised in 2002, itself drawing from lessons from the first seven reviews, remains sound but thin – more flesh needs to be put on its bones if the quality of both the process and its product is to be further improved.

Section 3: A brief comment on benchmarks

There have been a number of benchmarks to which international reviews have made reference. Further debate is required to explore those which appear to be most appropriate for use in relation to the youth policy reviews.

The report concludes with a number of overarching questions and some overarching recommendations. A full list of recommendations and the proposed new framework for thinking about youth policy in Europe comprise Appendices 1 and 2.

introduction

The Council of Europe international reviews of national 'youth policy' were set in train in 1996. Over the past decade, 14 such reviews have been conducted. Their purpose has been threefold:

- to advise on the national youth policy of the country under review;
- to draw lessons concerning youth policy from each national context for consideration by other countries;
- to develop a framework for youth policy that might guide the development of youth policy across the countries of the Council of Europe.

After the first seven reviews (of Finland, the Netherlands, Sweden, Spain, Romania, Estonia and Luxembourg) an expert review took place to reflect on the process to date, and a 'synthesis report' was produced. That synthesis report[3] drew together the substance of the available documentation (seven national reports (NRs) and seven international reports (IRs)) and proposed a developmental framework for subsequent reviews.

As a result of that reflection in 2002, both the process and the focus of the international reviews that followed were subject to greater rigour and consistency. Until that time, each international review had been conducted on a somewhat ad hoc and independent basis, though their common starting point had been the production of a national report by the country under review, which provided a basis for their deliberations. Moreover, each international review team had a similar composition. Routinely, they comprised three youth researchers (one serving as the rapporteur), a member of the secretariat and one member from each of the statutory bodies of the Youth Directorate of the Council of Europe (the CDEJ, the inter-governmental steering committee on youth, and the Advisory Council, representing youth organisations). Typically, the CDEJ member chaired the process. Though most reviews involved two visits to the country concerned, the direction of inquiry and subsequent analysis was left largely to the discretion of each international team. This, unsurprisingly, produced a pot pourri of findings and commentary, which were not in themselves readily comparable, though they did provide the basis for constructing an indicative framework within which future reviews might organise their deliberations.

In 1996, the idea of 'youth policy' remained relatively undeveloped. Over the next few years the countries reviewed advanced their own particular understanding

---

3. Williamson,H. (2002), *Supporting young people in Europe: principles, policy and practice*, Strasbourg: Council of Europe Publishing.

of the breadth and depth of 'youth policy'; the international review teams did likewise. By 2002, however, the idea of 'youth policy' had not only become more formed through the reviews themselves, but had become the subject of debate and development on other platforms. In particular, the European Union had produced, in 2001, its own White Paper on Youth.[4] And, following the synthesis report, the Council of Europe then published its own paper on standards for the development and implementation of youth policies in Europe.[5] This paper drew significantly, though not exclusively, on the analysis and argument of the synthesis report; it also took ideas from specific national contexts[6] and from parallel work that had been going on within the Council of Europe on youth policy indicators.[7]

There was, therefore, a growing body of knowledge about and around the idea of 'youth policy', together with a developing sense of an effective process within which international reviews of national youth policy should be carried out. This involved a preliminary visit by a senior member of the Youth Directorate, in order to establish specific areas of interest or concern for the country to be reviewed, to outline the desired framework for the production of the national report, and to prepare an agenda for the international visits. These requirements were not carved in stone and were subject to reflection and revision, but they assisted in producing an increasingly common practice for the review process. Moreover, the conclusions of the international review were to be subjected to an open national hearing in the country concerned as well as a formal presentation to the Joint Council of the Youth Directorate (the CDEJ and the Advisory Council), in either Strasbourg or Budapest.

This report does not seek to replicate the substantive depth of the first synthesis report. Rather, it is designed to consider a variety of issues emerging from a reading of the documentation from the second 'tranche' of seven country reviews (the national and international reports on Lithuania, Malta, Norway, Cyprus, Slovakia, Armenia and Hungary[8]). This includes suggestions concerning additions and modifications to the framework for youth policy first proposed in the 2002 synthesis report. It is also concerned with issues within youth policies that were not especially prominent in the first round of analysis, and with observations concerning the process of conducting the international reviews: questions of data capture and the quality of engagement, and the presentation and dissemination of findings.

It is timely, almost a decade since the first review (of Finland), to take a second 'overarching' look at the rationale for, and execution of, the international review process. It is hoped that this will help to further refine the practice of future reviews to further improve their meeting the three objectives outlined above.

---

4. European Commission (2001), *A new impetus for European youth: White Paper*, Brussels: European Commission.

5. European Steering Committee on Youth (CDEJ) (2003), *Select Committee of Experts on the establishment of guidelines for the formulation and implementation of youth policies*, Strasbourg: Council of Europe Youth Directorate.

6. For example, National Assembly for Wales (2000), *Extending Entitlement: supporting young people in Wales*, Cardiff: National Assembly for Wales.

7. Expert Group on Youth Policy Indicators (2003), *Final Report*, Strasbourg: Council of Europe Youth Directorate.

8. The designated rapporteur for the Hungary review contacted me in March 2006 to tell me that "the Hungary process has been completely postponed. ... the schedule is totally unclear at the moment". As a result, this report covers only six international reviews.

To this end, therefore, this paper has three components. First, drawing from the empirical material contained in the 'next six' national and international reports, suggestions will be made for building on the framework and issues proposed in the synthesis report which, of course, itself built on the empirical material from the first seven international reviews. Second, there will be some penetrating reflection from some of those who have been involved, in a variety of capacities, in those six international reviews, and an analysis of the recommendations they themselves have made for improving the process. Third, there will be some brief suggestions about the different benchmarks against which national youth policy may be appropriately 'tested' in terms of commentary within the subsequent international report. These ideas and themes are supplemented further by the reflections and deliberations that took place at a dedicated meeting of many of those who have been involved in the international review process, in Strasbourg in July 2006.[9]

9. See the report of the meeting by Dr Anthony Azzopardi, "International youth policy reviews, youth policy advisory missions and their impact on youth policy development in the Council of Europe".

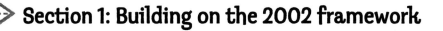

Section 1: Building on the 2002 framework

The synthesis report of 2002 drew exclusively from the seven national and international reports produced between 1997 and 2001 in order to construct a 'youth policy framework' that might inform a number of agendas: from cross-governmental thinking about standards for development and implementation, to the future production and presentation of international reviews.

Here, a reading of the next six national and international reports suggests that there are three ways of amending that initial provisional framework:

- the addition of new themes and issues;

- themes and issues that arguably demand more weight and attention;

- points within the main themes and issues requiring inclusion or a stronger focus.

Of the six countries under consideration, Malta, Cyprus and Armenia especially[10] have thrown into relief the fact that the framework originally established, though generally robust and still relevant, is imbalanced in terms of their country contexts and some issues are given either too little prominence or are conspicuous by their absence.

This section, therefore, is designed to rectify this situation. It will not repeat the content of the earlier report, which is available for comparative purposes, unless there is a specific reason for doing so. The 'insertions' made below must therefore be considered by reference to the framework outlined in the original synthesis report.

There is, before embarking on additions to that framework, the important question of gaps in knowledge, awareness and understanding. There was certainly at least an implicit statement in the international reports of Malta, Cyprus, Slovakia and Armenia that there were issues about which the international team would have

---

10. While of course there are many dissimilarities, Norway displays many similar features to Finland (both building on a distinctly Nordic tradition of youth policy), while Lithuania brings to its youth policy similar challenges to those facing its sister Baltic state, Estonia. Slovakia offers a perspective that is especially distinct, but nevertheless it still has strongly European resonances. Malta, Cyprus and Armenia present issues that are shared by at least two of these countries and are very different from any countries that have been subject to international youth policy reviews in the past: population size, being an island, conflict, the legacy and influence of religion, the general subordination of 'difference', and very pronounced colonial (Soviet or British in the 20th century) inheritance.

liked to have learned more, but did not.[11] Perhaps future reviews should be more explicit about such issues, with a dedicated section in the international report delineating them.

a. Concepts of 'youth' and 'youth policy'

This second synthesis report suggests that there are three new issues regarding 'youth' and three relating to 'youth policy' that demand further attention in future international reviews.

'Youth'

It always was a point of contention but attempts to produce a discrete definition of 'youth'[12] have now given way to debating the interlocking and overlapping of 'youth' in relation to 'childhood' and 'adulthood', and in the context of 'the family'. Put very crudely, children become 'youth' much earlier but remain in the category of 'youth' for much longer, particularly if the definition of youth rests on some level of dependency on family of origin. Moreover, Arnett's work on "emerging adulthood" (Arnett 2004) has provoked considerable theoretical debate about young people's capacity and opportunity to build, incrementally during their early twenties, what Bynner (2005) has described as "human, social and identity capital".

> There needs to be a place in national reports to describe and comment on the 'lived experiences' of different segments/sections of young people. The life and prospects of a university student in the capital are going to be very different from the young farm labourer in the countryside. Some case studies of 'my life' were requested during the Armenia review, but none was provided.

This shifting thinking about a range of transitions in prospect, experienced and 'managed' (in different ways) by young people clearly has implications for thinking about 'youth policy', especially its connections with 'childhood policy' and 'family policy'. Perhaps it is all the more significant, therefore, that the national youth report for Norway was the responsibility of, and produced by, the Ministry of Children and Family Affairs.

> There is, then, a new debate to be had about the separation and integration of 'youth' issues in relation to questions of childhood and family life.

Furthermore, there is, too often, an absence of a 'youth sociology' – drawing on theoretical and empirical data to set out the context and condition of (different groups of) young people in the society concerned. This was a point made explicitly by the international review of Armenia (Armenia IR p. 10), but it could have been made of many of the other reviews, with the exception of Norway, where the national report (Chapter 3) provides an excellent analysis of the contemporary condition and experiences of its young people. In particular, the issues identified concerning "autonomy or regulation" (Norway NR p. 23) are especially pertinent in considering

---

11. The international reports on Malta, Cyprus and Armenia – all significantly homogenous countries – raised the issue of minorities, while that for Slovakia (IR, p. 22) said the review team "would have liked to learn something about domestic violence, bullying in schools and lifestyle crimes".

12. This does, however, remain a point of contention in reporting procedures: for example, the national report of the Slovak Republic emphasises that there is still no legal concept of 'youth'. The attainment of 'adulthood' is either age 18 or marriage (Slovakia NR p. 7).

the backcloth to youth policy development, particularly whether they should relate to "interventionist or facilitative" approaches (Norway NR p. 12). More broadly, the Norway national report (p. 13) is quite clear about how its youth sociology provides the underpinning for its youth policy framework:

> The main goals of youth policy are, therefore, to help ensure that the resources represented by young people are focused on and utilized in important areas of society, and that the participation and influence of young people are promoted. The most important grounds for youth policy are presented as qualifying them to participate in society, in the widest sense. ... The cultural and leisure activities of young people are regarded as being both a part of such qualification and an opportunity for experience and recreation. In the leisure area, the term qualification means at least as much the acquisition of qualities such as initiative, self-management and self-control as the acquisition of knowledge and skills. ... the term digital competence is used to describe the ability of children and young people to make use of new media. ... it is important to develop such competence so that young people are able to utilize new educational services, and in order to prevent the emergence of new social dividing lines.

> A critically reflective analysis of the social condition of young people – a 'youth sociology' – should be strengthened as a component of national reports.

'Youth policy'

Formal youth policy – however designated in particular countries – is clearly not static. It is subject to preparation, political endorsement and then, at least theoretically, embedded for a specified future period. Whatever the volatility and instability of youth policy for reasons of political change, the notional administrative period for a particular phase of youth policy development has, arguably, been given insufficient consideration to date. If, however, the international review process is to build in a more formal 'follow-up' element (see below), then these time frames hold greater significance: they offer a clear signal about an appropriate moment for such a follow-up review. Slovakia, for example, has a youth policy development window from 2001 to 2007, while the strategy in Armenia has been approved for 2005-09.

> More explicit consideration should be given to the duration of contemporary phases of youth policy development in different countries, especially for both comparative purposes and in relation to a proposed 'follow-up' element in the international review process.

In similar vein, the more recent reviews throw into relief the different cycles of youth policy development in different countries and the length of a youth policy trajectory: in short, accounts of youth policy evolution. Cyprus (IR p. 22), for example, has had four "creation cycles", while Slovakia (NR pp. 12-14) talks of three phases. Armenia (draft NR pp. 16-17) also reports three distinct periods, one (1995-98) preparing the ground for a formal youth policy "Conception", the next (1998-2005) building up momentum and greater understanding and coherence, culminating beyond 2005 with a more confident and purposeful approach – which was, indeed, one of the reasons for seeking to participate in the international review process. All three of these countries, along with Lithuania, have relatively short stories to tell about linked phases of youth policy development,[13] in contrast to Norway which, with its first youth centre established in 1896 (NR p. 62), has a very long story to tell (for a very short version, see Norway IR pp. 15-16). Whether long or short, however, the evolutionary phases of youth policy in different countries need careful and clear reporting and explanation, both for comparative analysis and internal understanding.

> The evolution of national youth policy should be a stronger component of national reports, identifying distinct developmental phases and the reasons for them.

All countries face the continuing challenge of reconciling tradition and change, but such challenges appeared to be particularly acute in many of the nations under consideration. 'Youth policy' appeared to be struggling at the interface between a variety of still relatively solid traditions (education, community, family, church) and an equally varied cluster of modern influences (the Internet, Europe, sexual behaviour, immigration). As the Cyprus national report (p. 36), in conclusion to its chapter on the development of Cypriot society, observed:

> Thus, we all need to realize that we live in a transient society, where change is a constant phenomenon. Change cannot actually be prevented, it can be however, properly handled or managed. The big issue is the following: "What are we doing to prepare our youth for the range of alternative life-styles that are now developing?"

The specific challenges facing Armenia[14] highlighted the tensions at play between striving to affirm traditional culture and also aspiring to anticipate future culture:

> Even though Armenia has now endorsed its State Youth Policy Strategy, the debate on youth policy is in many ways just starting. ... And it is a debate that needs to establish the desired balance and interaction between an affirmative position that is characteristic of traditional Armenia and an anticipatory position that relates to the aspirations for an Armenia in the future. (Armenia IR p. 55)

> Both national and international reports need to pay attention to how 'youth policy' relates to the 'pathway' between tradition and change, and its position between affirmatory and anticipatory culture.

b. Structure and infrastructure

There are five issues here that are reinforced or re-emphasised by the reviews under consideration.

Legislation

The newness of formalisation of 'youth policy' is very striking in many of these countries. The much lauded Youth Policy Concept in Lithuania (in which the principle of co-management, now under threat, is enshrined) was approved only in 1996. Armenia's Conception on State Youth Policy was established in 1998 (though a draft Law was in process in 2005, according to Armenia IR p. 13). Slovakia has no

---

13. They do, of course, have a longer history of 'youth policy' but one of very different kinds.
14. It shares a past of Soviet control with other countries being considered here (Lithuania, Slovakia) but is distinguished from them in remaining close to Russia through membership of the CIS, in conflict and isolation, and experiencing levels of poverty more akin to the third world than to contemporary Europe.

youth law, but a Concept of State Policy towards children and young people (NR pp. 9, 13-14). Formal legislation has been viewed by some commentators[15] as an essential prerequisite to credible and committed state youth policy, yet it does not appear to have impeded progress and may sometimes be viewed as too much of a holy grail, demanding too much in the way of political (and financial) guarantees. And we should not forget that formal legislative provision for something as abstract as 'youth policy' remains very much the exception rather than the rule.

> We should perhaps not get too sidetracked by the assumption that youth policy will remain incoherent and slow in development in the absence of formal legislation. What demands critical evaluation is the strength of the mechanisms in place, be they legal or administrative.

Arms of the state or heads of a movement?

According to classical democratic positions, non-governmental organisations (NGOs) are precisely that: *non*-governmental, exercising their central place, independently, in civil society. Youth NGOs typically depict themselves in this way, yet this synthesis report identifies what might be described as a mixture of confusion and collusion. It is not, of course, possible to prescribe exactly what the relationship should, or needs to be between the state (government) and youth NGOs (civil society). That is a matter of eternal reflection in political science! Rather, here, some empirically derived points may be expressed, which may assist further deliberation and debate.

No country was immune from some expression of anxiety about the nature of the relationship between the state and youth organisations, and their representative body – the national youth council. And, whatever that relationship, one could assess it from different perspectives. Norway's children and youth council LNU, for example, was considered by some to be too close to government, a convenient and comfortable stepping stone to a job in the public administration. It was seen as too cosy. On the other hand, it could be seen as having established a shared platform for dialogue and a position of genuine influence through a mutually agreed framework.

The Slovakia national report (p. 11), reporting on its historical context, had the courage to observe that:

> One of the main political representatives at the time [1969] declared: "If we have a department of youth, we do not need youth organisations." He clearly evaluated the function of a youth organisation as a prolonged arm of government.

Yet this was precisely a concern expressed in the international review, given that Slovakia had, in 2000, subsumed its national youth council within a government ministry. It had done so for apparently the best of reasons:

> As of February 2000 the Slovak Youth Council became a partner organisation of the Slovak Ministry of Education, thus ending a period of unclear and changing relations between the representatives of the state on the one hand and the children's and youth organisations on the other … The status of an

15. For example, Peter Lauritzen, Director of Youth at the Council of Europe; his 'checklist' on the essentials of youth policy – including legislation – can be found in the Youth Policy Indicators report (*Final Report – Experts on Youth Policy Indicators*, Council of Europe Youth Directorate 2003, p. 10).

official partner enables it to fully participate on the planning and realisation of the national youth policy. (Slovakia NR pp. 122-23)

But this reasonable assertion did not stop the international report (p. 13) recommending that "A re-thinking of the role of the state, where youth organisations are rooted in civil society rather than in state-party structures, needs to be undertaken". Similarly, the international review of Malta (p. 89) suggested that civil society is under-developed: between the church and the state, it "does not have very much space within which to grow and develop". The same view was expressed in the international review of Armenia (p. 22), where certain youth organisations were considered to be part of a privileged 'inner circle' receiving resources from the state and not speaking out (against the government) on contentious issues – in return? The Armenian National Youth Council was alleged in some quarters to be 'too closed a club'.

Possibly the most contentious relationships at the time of any of the international reviews prevailed in Cyprus (reviewed 2004) when the status and role of the 'national youth council'[16] lacked clarity, especially in relation to the Cyprus Youth Board, which was often described as a 'semi-governmental organisation'. These matters have now been resolved, but it will be important for future international reviews to engage in more robust 'tests' of the composition, constitution and character of youth organisations and the national councils that theoretically represent them. Much has been made of the 'co-management' model established by Lithuania ("a space for the practice of youth initiative", NR p. 29), but even this was appearing vulnerable by 2006.

> Future international reviews need to explore more closely the nature of relationships between youth organisations, their national youth council and their government. Questions of independence and an authentic place in civil society are always a matter for debate and of perspective, but too much often seems to be taken for granted.

Budget and funding allocations

One of the most striking contrasts in all policy reviews is the resource base on which different governments are seeking to forge youth policy. Norway, as one might predict, directs quite phenomenally generous resources towards its young people (see NR p. 54). In contrast, Armenia, equally predictably, is desperately short of resources and still often 'donor-driven' (see IR p. 14). Yet, in relative terms, Armenia has witnessed significant additional resources for youth policy, though not as dramatic as the incremental growth of resources available to young people in Cyprus through the Cyprus Youth Board. Inevitably, there are always disputes about the most appropriate ways of allocating and distributing such resources. This was, paradoxically, especially contentious in Lithuania (see NR p. 29), despite the conditions of co-management.

> Making sense of the overall budget is one challenge for international reviews. Understanding how it is allocated – organisationally, geographically, on issues, and at what levels – is immensely complex. Yet documenting the absolute and relative allocations to young people in different countries is a challenge to which future international reviews must rise.

16. CyCIC – the Cyprus (Youth) Council for International Co-operation.

An 'arm's-length' national agency (for youth issues and affairs)

Most countries (and international organisations concerned with young people) agree that there is some kind of prima facie case for having a quasi-independent, 'arm's-length' national agency[17] for youth issues, youth policy and youth affairs. There are long-standing models in countries such as Finland (Alliansi), Sweden (Swedish Board of Youth Affairs) and England (National Youth Agency[18]). Apparently similar models have been established in Lithuania (State Council for Youth Affairs) and Cyprus (Cyprus Youth Board). Malta appears to have plans to establish its own National Youth Agency (IR p. 72). In contrast, Slovakia (NR p. 16) has a Government Council for Children and Youth that is not independent but is composed of both government and youth NGOs (like Lithuania's State Council for Youth Affairs). The Slovakia international report suggests, however, and without much detail, that it is "not functioning as intended" (IR p. 20). This observation does, nonetheless, capture a key question: what is intended in the formation and support of a national youth agency?

> Where national youth agencies at arm's length from government do exist, future reviews need to establish more clearly their roles, responsibilities and functions. What is the level and nature of their independence? How broad and deep are their responsibilities? To what extent does government exercise an influence over the strategic direction and content of their work?

A related issue concerning independent advocacy for young people is to do with the existence of an Ombudsperson or Commissioner for Children,[19] able to investigate and speak out with authority and autonomy. The first such post was established by Norway in 1981 (see IR p. 13). One is currently being proposed in Malta (see IR p. 10 and p. 60), and has recently been established in Armenia (see draft NR p. 145), though "this institution hasn't yet been rooted in Armenian society as an independent institution committed to human rights protection".

> Ombudspersons have tended to be associated with children and, as a result, perhaps somewhat overlooked when considering the position of young people. Yet they have the potential to play a key role in the protection of human rights and extension of opportunities for young people, and need more thorough attention within the review process.

Delivery of youth policy

The general assumption is that 'youth policy' is delivered through a cascading process from central to local levels and across a set of relationships between governmental and non-governmental organisations. This rather self-evident generality conceals, however, a very varied set of pract ices, to which material from the most recent reviews makes a further contribution.

Perhaps the most central question concerns the balance between centralised direction and local autonomy. There are strengths and weaknesses in both,

---

17. Not to be confused with 'national agencies' responsible for the administration and delivery of European Union youth programmes.

18. Though its counterpart in Wales, the Wales Youth Agency, which had been established in 1992, was closed down by ministerial decision in 2005. Its state (Welsh) funding was withdrawn and its functions subsumed within the Welsh Assembly Government.

19. 'Children' in these circumstances are defined within the UN Convention on the Rights of the Child as up to the age of 18.

but identifying where the power of youth policy strategy and delivery resides is essential to understanding its rationale and efficacy. The Norway international review (p. 94) highlights some tensions between central government aspirations and the considerable autonomy of the country's 434 municipalities, a point also made in relation to Slovakia (IR p. 31). In contrast, the Cyprus Youth Board takes a strong lead and is the key driver of youth policy, for which it receives considerable praise and support, despite some reservations (Cyprus IR p. 24).

There is an equally mixed position in relation to the place of youth organisations and national youth councils in youth policy delivery. There are, of course, the issues alluded to above concerning the limits to their autonomy and the breadth of their independent contribution, about which, for instance, Malta (IR p. 91) and Slovakia (IR pp. 23-24) provide useful commentary. There are further issues about the representativeness of national youth councils (see Slovakia IR p. 40) and their legitimacy (see Cyprus IR pp. 32-34) in speaking for young people and contributing to youth policy implementation. Both the national reports of Armenia (draft p. 113) and Slovakia (p. 122) indicate very limited participation in youth organisations.

Yet in Lithuania (NR pp. 48-52) it has been youth organisations that have been most significant in the delivery of youth policy for, although regional government has taken forward the youth policy agendas of central government, municipal government has been considered too ineffective to do so.

The common challenge for all countries lies in the co-ordination of youth policy development and delivery. Armenia (IR pp. 18-19) was generally complimented for achieving "reasonably significant developments in just two years, within a culture that appears resistant to change", while Cyprus (IR p. 23) has its Consultative Intra-Departmental Committee spanning the different ministries of the Republic of Cyprus Government. Norway (IR p. 25) has a policy committee of state secretaries, who meet monthly and are supported by a number of cross-departmental administrative working groups.

The first synthesis report suggested that part of the framework of youth policy was 'structures for delivery', both vertical and horizontal, and taking account of the role of youth organisations. This report suggests that greater attention needs to be paid to the organisation of 'delivery relationships' – how is youth policy taken forward and who is included within (and excluded from) the processes of decision-making as implementation shifts from central planning to local delivery.

---

c. Policy domains

The substantive framework suggested from the first synthesis report remains reasonably sustainable. There are, however, some additional themes within some of those policy domains that may require greater prominence and attention.

Education

Education is always a huge topic, within which the imminence of educational reform is almost ever-present. There is a new national curriculum in Malta (IR pp.38-39), Cyprus tabled reform proposals in 2004[20] (IR p. 35), and Armenia (draft NR p. 63) reported that

---

20. Educational Reform Committee (2004), *Democratic and Humanistic Education and Culture in the Eurocyprian State*, Nicosia, August 2004.

"Substantial changes and reforms in education are of critical importance as at present it is a top priority to educate a generation ready to meet the challenges of the future".

The reconstruction and modernisation of education is always, therefore, high on the youth policy agenda, but especially for countries undergoing dramatic and rapid transition and change. There are questions about structure and organisation, curriculum content, styles of learning and teaching, and questions of recognition and validation. There are also wider questions concerning inclusivity and dealing with the challenge of 'drop-out', and considerations of the place of non-formal education.

A trend can be detected in the gradual shift from authoritarian towards more democratic structures in education, as witnessed by, for example, students in Armenia sitting on the governing bodies of higher education institutions, and Schools Councils in Malta. Regarding the content of learning, there are still significant obstacles, often for religious reasons, to introducing more 'personal, health and social' issues in schools, beyond traditional academic subjects. This applies especially in Armenia and Cyprus, despite small glimpses of progress in this direction. Similarly, there is often resistance to the introduction of new pedagogy – new methods of teaching and learning. As the Armenia IR (p. 25) notes, "There still appears to be a firmly traditional pedagogy, one in which the teacher transmits knowledge, rather than one in which learners develop understanding". And, within an emergent European qualifications framework,[21] there are important issues – especially in the context of Armenia (see IR p. 24), with some 70 private and 20 public universities for a population of three million people – to do with the standards, quality and relevance of current educational provision.

All the reviews address the question of educational inclusion and new issues concerning drop-out and under-achievement. There are, in some countries, institutional fault lines that produce more division than necessary (see Malta IR p. 9) and different approaches to addressing exclusion and self-exclusion. Given the wider European agenda regarding the 'knowledge-based economy/society', these remain crucial issues for the attention of the international reviews.

Finally, most countries appear adept at expressing their commitment to the development of 'non-formal education' (especially to the Council of Europe!), but distinguishing between that rhetoric and any reality in terms of its practice is often difficult. Slovakia (NR p. 143) may be preparing to adopt the concept, but the Slovakia IR (p. 26) reports an official as saying "the Slovak Republic does not understand the meaning of the concept of non-formal learning / education – but it is being practised". Armenia (draft NR pp. 71-72), likewise, may be preparing a concept document, but the draft national report (p. 69) admits to little awareness of non-formal education and comments that it is often viewed as "not serious and ridiculous" (p. 71). Even Norway (IR p. 47) is not particularly explicit about its reasons for commitment to non-formal education; somehow it just happens!

> In addressing educational issues, international reviews need to ensure (1) a close focus on (a) structure and organisation, (b) content, (c) delivery, and (d) standards. They also need to give attention to (2) drop-out, inclusion and achievement. Finally, they need to unravel (3) the real understanding and practice of the concept of non-formal education.

21. See Commission of the European Communities (2006), *Implementing the Community Lisbon Programme: Proposal for a Recommendation of the European Parliament and of the Council on the Establishment of the European Qualifications Framework for Lifelong Learning*, Brussels, 5 September 2006.

Section 1: Building on the 2002 framework

Training and employment

Both the Malta NR (p. 85) and the Slovakia IR (p. 37) took up the definitional issues between, on the one hand, 'employability' and, on the other, 'employment prospects'. These relate, of course, to labour market supply and demand. Countries cannot depend on training programmes to improve the skills and competencies of young people if there is no demand side for them.

Wider social questions now have to be connected to narrow labour market issues around training and employment. These include the increasing disillusionment, alienation and sometimes despair of young people who have been subjected to the 'revolving door' of labour market 'activation programmes' – without success. There is growing evidence that such measures are not likely to have a significant effect on inserting more vulnerable and marginalised young people into secure and sustainable employment (Walther and Stauber 2002). Thus, attention needs to turn to the extent, emergence and acceptance of what has been called 'sliced life' – various combinations for living, earning and learning – and youth policy support for this more flexible menu (Malta NR p. 91).

Within this new framework of 'sliced life', greater attention therefore also needs to be given to training and working beyond official structures. Both Armenia (draft NR p. 31, IR p. 28) and Malta (IR p. 53) appear to have expanding activity in 'non-formal employment' and the twilight economy, as well as, alongside Cyprus, continuing economic dependency, engagement and possibly exploitation within the context of family enterprise. Yet, while families provide some interim economic support, young people in Armenia and Cyprus (NR p. 88) appear to be seeking security within the public sector and political administration – despite requiring more and more qualifications to achieve this. Such 'qualification inflation' (Cyprus NR p. 90, Armenia IR p. 27) remains a major issue for many countries.

Finally, given this increasing need for young people to 'juggle' a range of commitments and aspirations, the reliability of any data concerning participation levels in education and the labour market in contrast to youth unemployment has to be called into question. They become more and more a statement about the method of collection, rather than any dependable guide to reporting on the actual situations of the young people concerned.

> Training and employment – once a clear alternative for young people who ceased to be engaged in education – has now become muddled, muddied and mixed with other activity, as young people opt, or are forced, to create their own individualised version of 'sliced life'. More hidden economic activity is likely to be taking place, both in the labour market and in the domestic arena. Future international reviews will need to explore these complexities more carefully.

Health

International reviews need to avoid being trapped into a disproportionate focus on substance misuse and the use of illegal drugs. There is a far greater 'panorama' of health issues that demand attention. Yet Cyprus (NR p. 78) and Slovakia (NR pp. 96-99) appear overpreoccupied with drug abuse, just as Norway (IR p. 55) seemed unable to differentiate between different forms of abuse and addiction. The Slovakia IR (p. 23) makes the pertinent observation that in revisiting priority risk behaviours "what tops the list?".

In most countries it is certainly not illegal drugs, even if this commands media anxiety and political concern. Physical health, especially changes in diet as a result of commercialism and consequent levels of obesity, should be of far greater concern. Only Armenia and northern Cyprus (where there is no McDonalds – see Cyprus IR p. 44) would appear to be sustaining traditional healthy diets; elsewhere, there are major concerns about physical health, especially in Malta (NR p. 69, p. 73), where nearly a quarter of young people aged 10 are obese.

Beyond physical health concerns, other health priorities are sexual health (especially in rapidly modernising countries) and mental health problems arising from a sense of social dislocation (Rutter and Smith 1995). Cyprus (NR p. 75) and Malta (NR p. 63) both report the fatalities amongst young men through road accidents, while Slovakia (NR pp. 99-100) suggests that gambling addiction is an issue that is routinely overlooked.

Beyond the 'evidence' about the nature and balance of health issues among young people in different countries, there is then the question of health policy and the extent to which there are dedicated youth health services. Lithuania (NR p. 113), for example, has established six centres of youth health, while UNICEF in Armenia (IR, pp. 31-32) is piloting a sexual health education programme in a small number of schools. Where such provision does exist, however, there are questions around the personal and cultural barriers to making use of it. Indeed, the twin issues of awareness and access (see Armenia draft NR p. 98) are a critical focal point if international youth policy reviews are to evaluate the success of health initiatives directed at young people.

> Concerns about illegal drug use should not overshadow wider, and usually more prevalent, health concerns. Beyond prevalence issues, there is also the need to focus on the range of dedicated youth health services available and the extent to which young people are aware of, and make use of them.

Values and religion (the church)

Though this was a feature of the earlier synthesis report, it was probably given insufficient prominence. The Armenian Apostolic Church exercises a sustaining influence on young people in Armenia (draft NR p. 75, IR p. 40) and its history remains a core curriculum subject in Armenian schools. The spiritual influence of the Greek Orthodox Church in the Republic of Cyprus may have waned to some extent, but its role in social and community life is not diminished (Cyprus IR p. 52). The Roman Catholic Church remains "profoundly influential in Maltese life" (Malta IR p. 71), serving as a role model for many young people.

> The place of religion in the contemporary lives of young people – whether as the basis for values or as the mechanism for social and community integration – has perhaps been underestimated. Future reviews should give it greater attention.

Leisure and culture

As in the case of religion, the sustaining influence of traditional culture has, arguably, been rather overlooked. There are three issues here. First, particularly in countries such as Cyprus (IR pp. 47-48) and Armenia (IR p. 35), the persistence of traditional dance and music remains significant in the lives of contemporary youth. Attention needs to be paid both to young people's cultural heritage and to their 'modernity' and cultural creativity. Second, there is an important question concerning the distribution of access to leisure-time opportunities for different groups of young people (see, for example, Armenia IR p. 36). Third, and perhaps of most significance, is the declining access to leisure for all young people. Far from the hedonistic youth cultures sometimes claimed to characterise young people in western Europe, evidence from countries such as Armenia, Cyprus and Slovakia suggests that so-called 'leisure' time is taken up increasingly with improving personal chances of formal educational achievement. In Armenia (IR, pp. 35-36), young people said they were always studying and had little time for unstructured leisure; in Cyprus (IR p. 40), young people seemed to be absorbed into 'coaching classes', while the Slovakia NR (p. 83) observes:

> They devote more and more energy and time to the growth of their own professional competency. Its requirements also influence the choice of leisure time activities.

Future international reviews need to be conscious of (a) the use of leisure time for both traditional and modern culture, (b) issues concerning unequal access to leisure-time activities, and (c) the contraction of leisure time in the interests of enhancing formal learning and qualification.

Military and alternative service

The early international youth policy reviews said little about military service and its alternatives (and nor have the reports on Norway and Slovakia in this round of analysis); where they did, the issues were generally relatively unproblematic. Service was 'routine' in peacetime conditions and reasonable alternatives were available for those objecting to perform it on the grounds of conscience. Such circumstances also prevail in Lithuania (NR pp. 122-23), where youth work is a priority area for the Ministry of Defence, where training and education are made available during military service, and where there is flexibility around the performing of military service. Few have applied for, and even fewer permitted to undertake, alternative service (Lithuania NR p. 124).

The situation is very different, however, in Armenia and Cyprus, both countries in conditions of conflict where the idea of alternative service is still often perceived – and was previously treated – as akin to desertion and a crime (see, for example, Armenia draft NR p. 138). Though alternative service (both in uniform without a weapon, and through community service) is now available in both countries, it does not correspond to the standards of the Council of Europe (see Cyprus IR p. 51, and Armenia IR pp. 38-39). The duration of alternative service is too long and the conditions, in Armenia (IR p. 39), are often intolerable.

There are, then, some important issues concerning both the timing and conditions of military service and the duration, content and conditions, and consequences of alternative service. Cyprus (NR p. 175 and IR p. 38), for example, has recently given attention to improving conditions for young conscripts and established computer training for soldiers. The Armenia IR (p. 40) recommends similar measures there.

Military service remains a significant feature in young people's lives in some countries, though with different meanings and risks. It is, equally, a significant feature of 'youth policy' in some countries, though again within different priorities and with different objectives. The nature of alternative service possibilities reflects the different political contexts in which it is available. This synthesis report confirms its place within the repertoire of youth policy initiatives: as the Armenia draft NR (p. 138) notes, the army is the biggest youth organisation in Armenia and commands the greatest level of trust amongst young people.

Family policy and child welfare

The international reviews still do not provide sufficient information on this policy domain, although they should do, given the broad research evidence of increasingly protracted dependency of young adults on their families, and the responsibility given increasingly to families to keeping their children 'in good shape'. As young people remain for longer within their families of origin and become more dependent on family support (for which the national reports of Lithuania, Cyprus and Armenia provide some evidence), the structure of 'family life' is changing dramatically, especially in countries such as these, which are moving rapidly from tradition to modernity.

There are, furthermore, issues concerning the impact on such 'family life' (in both families of origin and families of destination) of migratory working needs. The frequent or longer-term absence of young people – as both 'children' and parents – is referred to in both the Slovakia NR (p. 73) and the Armenia IR (pp. 47-48).

Despite these ramifications of wider circumstances on family life, the family remains, in virtually all countries, a 'private realm' (see, for example, Norway IR p. 13) where external intervention should be very limited and which should continue to carry a range of responsibilities in terms of 'human socialisation'. As a result of this view of the family as the 'foundation stone of society' (Armenia IR p. 34), this has sometimes deterred youth policy from addressing certain key issues within other policy domains. The sexual health needs of young people in Armenia (draft NR p. 41, and IR p. 31) are a case in point.

Future international reviews need to pay more attention to the family context and family policy. This is imperative given the overwhelming general evidence about extended youth transitions and greater sustained 'attachment' to families of origin. It is also important given the increasingly migratory working habits of young adults in relation to both families of origin and destination. And the 'sanctity' of family life and responsibility has to be reflected upon in terms of how this may inhibit important policy activity both within the family and beyond it in other policy domains.

Housing

This is another relatively neglected area of youth policy, the importance of which has been reinforced in more recent international reviews. The earlier international review of Spain was correct in predicting that the housing needs of young people would soon become a major youth policy challenge.

There are, of course, new relations being established between extended families – being parents and their young adult children. Many young people in Cyprus, Malta and Armenia who remain longer in their families of origin do not experience any significant 'problems'. This does not mean, though, that alternatives – if they were available – would not be preferable. Young people may not feel 'trapped', but their situation may be no more than tolerated. Therefore it is important to address the desirable housing needs of young people and to explore what kind of housing is available, especially in relation to both affordability and accessibility. There are clearly new initiatives needed to respond to new circumstances. Norway (IR p. 63) has adapted its Husbanken grants and loans schemes, Armenia (IR p. 33) is exploring a mortgage lending scheme through its State Insurance Fund, and the international report on Malta (IR p. 65) makes a number of proposals in relation to the unoccupied property that exists there.

There are, inevitably, tensions that will always exist in housing policy – between younger and older generations, between the private and more 'public' sectors, and between rental arrangements and owner occupation.

> The international review process has a key role in gathering robust data on housing issues affecting young people. These concern the housing status of young people, their aspirations, access to affordable independent living, and mechanisms for supporting housing transitions.

Youth justice

Many of the national reports (for example, Cyprus NR p. 127, Norway NR pp. 68-69) allude to the changing profile of youth offending in their countries in terms of volume, patterns and perpetrators. There is often an implicit insinuation that the scale and character of youth crime is a consequence of multiculturalism and immigration. And though Norway's progressive approach to dealing with young offenders now encounters new difficulties (see IR pp. 61-63), other countries had youth justice systems that could only be described as anachronistic (Cyprus IR p. 49, Armenia IR pp. 37-38). In these countries (and Malta) there are clearly problems of economies of scale; there are relatively few young offenders for separate provision to be viable. Thus, in Cyprus (NR p. 126), juvenile offenders continue to be incarcerated alongside adults.

Whether or not a retributive or reformative ethos prevails, the coherence of youth justice measures in particular countries in relation to wider youth policy objectives and practice merits critical reflection, as indeed does the range of measures available for responding to an increasingly complex picture of offending by young people.

> Future international reviews should map the changing profile of youth offending and consider the coherence of youth justice responses in relation to wider youth policy, as well as exploring the range of interventions available for the character and severity of that offending profile.

d. Cross-cutting issues

In the first synthesis report, some key 'cross-cutting' issues were distilled from the 14 reports examined. This synthesis report confirms and consolidates the validity of those issues but the more recent reviews also bring into the picture more clearly other cross-cutting issues. These were not absent in the earlier reports but their prominence was not sufficiently strong to merit inclusion – at that time – in the initial framework of youth policy. There is now a much stronger case for their inclusion.

i) Confirming and developing those in the first report

Youth participation and citizenship

The Malta IR (p. 8) confirms the need within youth policy to construct a balance between youth support and youth autonomy.[22] The latter, however, is certainly assisted by structures for youth participation and those that facilitate the practice of citizenship. Though youth NGOs remain important, there is not always a great deal of trust in them in some societies (Armenia draft NR p. 113). Youth participation may, however, as the Malta IR (p. 29) suggests, also be promoted and supported through young people's social commitment and voluntary activities (see also Williamson and Hoskins 2005). Furthermore, as the Slovakia NR (p. 35, p. 128) points out, youth participation is not just a leisure-time option, nor even just a civic contribution, but a learning platform that enhances a range of "transversal skills".

So while there remains some fierce debate about the meaning and purpose of 'participation' (Slovakia NR p. 114), there is little doubt that the repertoire of possible routes to citizenship is underdeveloped in most countries. Cyprus (IR p. 56), for example, is keen to strengthen support for young people's social and civic engagement, though the concept of 'volunteering' remains somewhat abstract. Even a country such as Norway (NR pp. 91-100), with a huge commitment, long history and broad experience of encouraging youth participation, is still challenged by the task, as the Norway IR (p. 65) observed:

> Many county youth councils seem to be dormant or non-existent. Indeed, for a country with such a level of political and financial commitment to participation, gaps such as these came as some surprise to the international review team.

> Youth participation and citizenship may be a fundamental cross-cutting theme but it remains a challenge across the spectrum of possible 'facilitating' contexts and activities; it is at different stages in different countries, and it can mean very different things. The important point for the international reviews is to document the repertoire of opportunities, experiences and initiatives that are considered to assist these outcomes.

Social inclusion

The more countries that are reviewed, the more it becomes evident that very different notions of 'exclusion' and 'inclusion' prevail. By the standards of some western European countries, it could be argued that the majority of people in Armenia are excluded. However, a more relativistic position is equally problematic, for different reasons. Rapporteurs of international reviews may have to be 'creative'

---

22. The European Union White Paper *A New Impetus for European Youth* talks of promoting greater autonomy for youth, but this would be contested by broader research evidence which points up the need for greater support for young people in a general environment of risk and vulnerability.

on the subject (as some have already been), but they need some anchor points. One useful starting point in the academic literature might be Levitas (2005).[23]

Within the reviews, some persist with the concept of poverty: the Malta IR (p. 59) suggests that 15% of the population fell below the 'at risk of poverty' line, while around 50% of the population of Armenia (IR p. 4) are defined as living in poverty. Norway (IR p. 65) has its own notion of 'exclusion', which relates primarily to early school drop-out, worsening health issues and changing patterns of criminality.

So the word 'exclusion' is on many lips, and it inevitably produces strategies for inclusion. Slovakia (NR, p. 27), for example, has a National Action Plan for Social Inclusion. In the evolution of the Council of Europe reviews, however, awareness of the disadvantages of, and sometimes discrimination against, certain social groups has produced a position that is primarily concerned with structures for access and inclusion. In other words, while attention can remain focused on, for example, the Roma in Slovakia (IR pp. 39-40) or people with disabilities in Armenia (draft NR p. 51), the policy focus could readily shift to the measures for assisting access and enabling greater inclusion. Whether these are – to invoke Levitas' framework – redistributive fiscal measures (such as grants for learning), social integration measures (such as vocational training programmes) or remoralisation strategies (such as compulsory training for parents), the point is to consider them against wider international standards and assess them for their subjective credibility.

> Rather than dwell on academic definitions of 'exclusion' (which will be endless) or seek to pinpoint specific excluded groups of young people, the 'social inclusion' focus of the international reviews should be on public strategies for access and inclusion. Reviews should reflect on their efficacy from both an international and subjective perspective.

Youth information

Article 13 of the United Nations Convention on the Rights of the Child is concerned with the right to information. But although we may live in an 'information society', the scale, nature and availability of information varies considerably from country to country and, significantly, within countries. Public policy efforts to compensate for 'information inequalities' that may exist in the domestic arena reflect the huge international divide in terms of resources, understanding and approach. Norway (IR p. 66) has an impressive government-run web page to supplement other youth information services, which in turn supplement the Internet access available in schools and in at least three-quarters of homes. Cyprus (IR p. 58) has impressive Youth Information Centres in Nicosia and Larnaca and the Cyprus Youth Board intends to develop this network. Contrast these positions to Armenia's (IR p. 46) valiant attempt to disseminate information through a government-supported youth newspaper; as the Armenia draft NR (p. 134) notes, there are 'significant roadblocks' to establishing better youth information services, though there are plans afoot for such developments in television and through the proposed regional youth centres.

There is, therefore, the 'top-down' question of information provision. There is also, however, the 'bottom-up' question of how young people make use of information.

---

23. Levitas maintains that the three primary discourses around poverty and social exclusion are the classical socialist Redistributive Discourse (RED), a more recent Social Integrationist Discourse (SID) that has been embraced under the 'third way', and a Moral Underclass Discourse (MUD) favoured by the new right. She then examines these in the context of Britain's new Labour under Tony Blair.

Only half of young people in Armenia (draft NR p. 64) have access to the Internet, and television remains the main source of information for most young people (Armenia draft NR p. 68).

> This synthesis report confirms the need to explore youth information through both the services available and the ways in which they are (or are not) used by young people.

Multiculturalism and minorities

It is easy to observe that most modern societies are composed of people from multiple and diverse ethnic backgrounds, but this is not in fact always the case. Armenia (IR p. 3), for example, is a "significantly mono-ethnic, monothetic and monolingual society".[24] There are, of course, a range of very specific reasons for this. Indeed, the greater 'multiculturalism' that prevails in other countries has many different roots and antecedents. On a spectrum from most to least diverse, the recent international reviews could be characterised as follows:

> Malta's historical mix > Cyprus (GCs, TCs, Turks and others*) > Armenia > Norway post-Norwegianisation > Lithuania / Slovakia

*Greek Cypriots, Turkish Cypriots, Turkish settlers and others

What emerges from the international reviews is the need for a far more calibrated and sophisticated definition of, and reflection on the idea of 'minorities'. There are the 'indigenous people' of Norway, the 'national minorities' of Norway and the 'minor religious' groups of Cyprus, old immigrants and new immigrants, refugees and asylum-seekers, sexual minorities. Some such groups (the Sami in Norway, the Roma in Slovakia) have received a high profile in the youth policy debate, some have remained completely invisible (all but Cypriots in the Cyprus review – IR pp. 61-62). Indeed, the Malta IR (p. 44) expresses frustration about such invisibility, regretting that there was no opportunity to meet minority groups and therefore an inability to comment on their treatment and experiences.

Norway (NR p. 72) is clear that it seeks to make the issues concerning an increasingly multicultural country transparent. Other countries are more reticent about their 'accommodation' of both older and newer minorities.

> Future international reviews need not only distil the specific complexities of multiculturalism within the particular country under review but also endeavour to make contact with less visible 'minority' groups of young people to explore their experiences.

Mobility and internationalism

The first synthesis report suggested mobility and internationalism as a cross-cutting issue largely in relation to student mobility, InterRailing and other positive aspects of an enlarging and connected Europe. The focus at that time was certainly not on migration, and definitely not on enforced migration.

---

24. The Armenia NR (p. 82) would wish to challenge this by pointing to the 11 different minority groups who live in Armenia, all with an equal chance of making a life there.

Like 'multiculturalism', however, mobility functions at different levels and across a spectrum from substantial benefits to serious challenges. It is said that some of the countries recently reviewed are "ambivalent Europeans" (Malta IR p. 31), wishing to secure the benefits of the European Union but hoping to avoid what are perceived to be some of its negative consequences. Within particular countries, there are huge challenges in relation to internal mobility and migration, both voluntary and – in the case of Armenia's displaced population – compelled.

Thus it is a complex picture: internal migration from the countryside to the cities, movement for studying within and beyond national borders (some returning, some not), mobility for temporary or permanent employment away from 'home' (sometimes legal, sometimes not), the trafficking in women, and access to the mobility programmes of the European institutions.

Armenia (draft NR p. 26 and pp. 42-43) experienced phenomenal immigration and emigration during the 1990s: some 400,000 immigrants as a result of the conflict with Azerbaijan, and around 1 million emigrants because of the volatile economic and political situation. Cyprus (IR p. 12) now provides an entry point to the European Union and is increasingly concerned about the illegal trafficking in migrants, drugs and women. Internally, as the political tensions between the north and south of the island ease somewhat, increasing numbers of Turkish Cypriots cross the Green Line each day for work (Cyprus IR, p. 38). Such mobility for employment, over weeks and months rather than on a daily basis, is commonplace amongst Armenians, who go for work in Ukraine and Belarus (Armenia IR p. 47). And though the Lithuanian review took place before Lithuania's entry to the EU, there is anecdotal evidence that some 20% of the population moved west (apparently for work) in May 2004. There are, further, deep concerns about migration for work in the illegal economies of other countries. This may be a quasi-voluntary decision but, equally, it may be enforced, for example in the trafficking, especially from and through Armenia, of young women (Armenia IR pp. 47-48, draft NR pp. 147-49).

In terms of young people, there are significant mobility questions concerning education. While Cypriots from both the south and north of the divided island often go abroad to pursue their higher education, it is far less common for Turkish Cypriots in the north to return, whereas Greek Cypriots from the south tend to come home (Cyprus IR, p. 63). Many young people from Norway elect to study abroad, just as students from other countries seek to study in Norway (NR pp. 103-5). This issue here, therefore, is twofold: the prevalence of young people studying away from their country of origin, and the proportions who return.

The European institutions, particularly the European Union YOUTH programme,[25] have placed a great deal of significance on mobility and internationalism to promote learning exchange and intercultural learning. There are, therefore, further questions concerning the attachment of young people to such exchange programmes, the multiplier or cascade effects of that experience, and the access to such programmes for different groups of young people. For quite different reasons, some young people who are eligible to participate in such programmes face significant barriers in doing so. Young people from northern Cyprus (IR p. 64) and from Armenia (draft NR pp. 154-55, IR p. 48) do so, for related but rather different reasons.

---

25. The YOUTH programme was concerned with youth exchanges, study visits by professional youth workers, the European Voluntary Service Programme, and youth initiatives; it is now called the Youth in Action Programme, running from 2006 to 2013.

All such mobility processes and practices have knock-on effects for wider policy: the demographic and generational balance, the skills base, and the sustaining or changing of prevailing political orientations.

> Mobility and internationalism are, self-evidently, more than studying abroad and InterRailing. Their complexity needs to be unravelled during international reviews, especially in terms of education and employment, coerced migration, whether or not people return or stay, and access to and barriers concerning European programmes.

Equal opportunities

The Slovakia NR (p. 112) observes that "In reality, the position of women in the Slovak society isn't quite as idealistic as it is declared in the mentioned norms", and much the same can be said of both Cyprus (IR pp. 64-65) and Armenia (IR pp. 49-50). At least the national reports from these countries said something about gender equality issues. This was not the case in relation to sexual minorities and gay rights – which were completely ignored by Malta, Cyprus and Armenia, and subject to the following remark by Slovakia (NR p. 110): "There are no laws in Slovakia that would create a legislative basis against sexual minorities' discrimination". The same applies to Armenia (IR p. 50). In Cyprus (IR p. 65), an individual's driving licence is automatically revoked for those who do not serve in the army for 'psychological reasons' (a euphemism for homosexuality). At least Malta's international report contained an addendum giving a voice to the Malta Gay Rights Movement.

> There is plenty of lip service to equal opportunities. International reviews need to explore beyond issues of gender equality and consider the position of young people with disabilities and different sexual orientation who have, to date, been given insufficient explicit attention in the process.

ii) Emergent issues demanding a stronger emphasis

Radicalisation / reaction v. conformity

There is still not a great deal of attention in either national or international reports to 'extremism' among young people and any policy response – which could clearly range from efforts at understanding and accommodation to crackdowns and suppression. Any response would necessarily be informed by the nature of the alleged or evidenced extremism. It would also, almost certainly, be located within the context of political anxieties about fundamentalism and reaction, and linked to aspirations around democratic inclusion and renewal.

Norway's national report dedicates a short section to 'Nationalist youth groups', which makes the telling point (NR p. 74) that:

> The growth of and recruitment to these groups is a serious problem, both for the children and young people who become involved in such movements and for their families and local communities.

Slovakia's national report, likewise, discusses briefly 'Extremist groups', including those that have promoted "the ideology of the pro-Nazi state in Slovakia during the WWII" (NR p. 101). Racially motivated crime has increased significantly over the past 10 years.

Both reports speak to the resurgence of old racisms and extremisms (in particular white supremacist neo-Nazi groups) and do not address concerns about new forms of radicalism and fundamentalism. We should, however, anticipate this issue becoming more prominent in future reviews.

> Though discussion remains sparse, it is likely that future reviews will need to give greater attention both to the resurgence of old forms of racism and extremism and new forms of radicalism and fundamentalism.

Local v. global pressures

The national reports of Malta, Cyprus and Armenia are especially forthright in their expression of the tensions around seeking the preservations of traditional values (see also 'Leisure and culture' above) in the face of intrusion and encroachment by (more liberal) global and European values. Even the Slovakia NR (p. 102) observes in relation to the emergence of more extremist youth groups (see above): "One area of tension is where local patriotism is confronted with the globalisation pressures ...".

> The 'glocal' mantra favoured by youth cultural theorists and internationalists may conceal much sharper tensions, even conflicts, between sustaining local tradition and embracing global influences. How this is managed and experienced in the lives of young people may be a useful focus for the international policy reviews.

New technologies

Nowhere is the potential tension between tradition and modernity more apparent than in relation to new technologies. They represent both cultural invasion and, for some, a form of cultural rescue: "young people prefer flexible, fast and frivolous communication" (Slovakia NR p. 25).

There is a huge set of questions here, around issues such as access, usage, and location – the use of new technologies by young people and their use for youth policy. There is a rapidly expanding academic literature about the multiple uses of the mobile phone in the lives of young people. The Internet clearly provides myriad opportunities for learning and engagement, as well as more leisure-based, even sinister activities.

Malta appears to be particularly committed to 'rolling out new technology to schools' (IR p. 45) and to develop technology education and learning through technology. Armenia's position on this front, in contrast, is very weak – over half of young people have no access to the Internet (NR p. 64). Lithuania, though starting from a similar position only a few years ago (the IR p. 30 suggests the education system "falls far short of European standards"), has embarked on systematic reform of its education system which recognises the need for technological investment in learning (NR pp. 74-76). And though Lithuania sees the importance of close links between schools and the information society, the Slovakia NR (p. 32) reports that "The so-called 'new technologies' play currently only a marginal role in the dissemination of information in the rights of young people". One in eight young people did not use a computer at home or at school, and this, predictably, adversely affected their educational performance (Slovakia NR p. 50). These data were from 2003 and the situation has probably changed considerably. Nevertheless, it is clear that there remains a significant digital divide both between and within countries, which may be compounded by, for example, a gender divide in the use of new technologies (Malta IR pp. 42-43). Norway, as one might presume, is already fully up to speed!

> Given the critical impact of new technologies both in the lives of young people and in the framework for the delivery of youth policy, they merit considerably more analysis in future reports than they have received in the past.

Centre–periphery

Related to the "old" cross-cutting issue concerning mobility, and the emergent theme of local/global pressures (above) and urban/rural debates (see below), is a clear policy anxiety in many countries about the ways to address disparities between the 'centre' and the 'periphery'. Concretely, this usually means between the capital city and the regions. The former is attractive to young people for reasons of both leisure and learning: it is 'where the action is'. The archetypal situation is perhaps in Norway, where strikingly multicultural Oslo is dramatically different from the sustaining homogeneity elsewhere in the country(side). And though there is a policy of 'dispersal' of arriving ethnic minorities throughout the 434 municipalities, many if not most subsequently return to Oslo (see IR p. 74). For this and other reasons, a strong regional policy that, critically, includes youth policy dimensions, has been developed. Similar challenges can be detected in other countries. Cyprus (IR p. 58) is seeking to extend its youth information services to smaller communities. Slovakia has established its Regional Youth Information Centres (ICM – see NR pp. 132-3) and regional leisure time centres (IR p. 25). Armenia is in the process of developing regional youth centres (IR p. 18), which is described as an "unprecedented programme" in the draft national report (p. 18).

> The international reviews have tended to focus on national and then local youth issues, arguably to the neglect of regional questions. More exploration and debate are required about relationships between the centre and the periphery, especially with regard to regional (youth) strategies concerned with issues such as migration, information, leisure and culture, as well as key infrastructure dimensions such as education, employment and housing.

Urban–rural polarisation

A related version of the centre–periphery question is that of urban–rural polarisation: the drift of young people (often the more able, motivated and qualified) away from rural communities to the cities. Thus not only may a regional strategy be needed (see above) but also a rural strategy. This is apparent in the Norway IR (pp. 81-82), which builds on the observation in the NR (p. 82) that employment opportunities (usually given as the reason for leaving) are by no means enough: there needs to be a "full range of services and facilities". Clearly, very small communities cannot provide such a range alone, and therefore there are always key questions of transport and communications if access to such provision is to be achieved. Lithuania's 'yellow bus' policy (NR p. 78) in relation to the transportation of pupils to school is a case in point. Internet-based teaching and learning programmes, such as those being developed in Norway (IR p. 81), are another. The crunch will always be about appropriate and attractive methods of taking services to young people and, where this is not possible, taking young people to services, using both physical and virtual means.

> The pace of 'urbanisation' of most societies is unlikely to slow down but it does have huge implications for the sustainability of rural communities – their economies, leisure infrastructure and demographic balance in particular. Young people have a central place in these trends – they are more likely to leave but, conversely, it will be their enterprise that will revive the countryside. This has been a somewhat neglected discussion in the international reviews to date.

Elites and outsiders

Beyond geographical shifts and drifts (mobility and migration), there is a matter of social mobility or its absence through the preservation of social and occupational privilege. This has not been apparent (or at least not mentioned) in the early international reviews, but it was reported, albeit with some humour, in relation to Malta (IR p. 27):

> One of the paradoxes of this small and intimate total society, however, is that the social distance between the elite and the grassroots seems to be the same – in relative terms – as one might find in larger, more complex and pluralistic societies. One of the perennial complaints the review team heard concerned the elite allegedly being out of touch with the ordinary people. Initially some of us marvelled that it was possible to be out of touch with anyone in Malta, but there did appear to be some truth in this assertion.

There are, of course, different forms and manifestations of 'elitism'. However, in a number of reviews (Cyprus, Armenia, Lithuania in particular), there were glimpses of some such processes developing within the youth policy context. There was a privileged 'inner circle' (from politics, NGOs and elsewhere) considered by outsiders to be self-serving and defending its advantages and connections (the links between government, NGOs and key individuals). The 'outsiders' remained unaware or ill-informed of resources, initiatives and action. Though there was sometimes attention to these concerns – in terms of, for example, recruitment to and composition of committees, or procedures for the allocation of public-sector grants – it was not always clear how serious this was, or whether it remained somewhat tokenistic.

> Youth policy development is not immune from the normal evolution of political bureaucracy, whereby early 'insiders' consolidate their positions and, in time, form a privileged elite at the expense of latecomers and outsiders. Robust scrutiny of such situations would seem to be an important role for the international reviews.

Environmental issues

On a quite different front, a greater focus on environmental issues seems now to be demanded. Early reviews usually raised the environment only in the context of 'single-issue' political commitment by young people. There is now, throughout country populations, a general commitment to raise awareness of environmental challenges and educate young people about environmental responsibility. The Cyprus Youth Board (NR p. 176) places considerable emphasis on this front, as does the Slovakia Government (NR pp. 27-28), though the Slovakia IR (p. 22) did feel its 'environmental education' programme was too formal and represented a real opportunity to apply more non-formal learning methodologies.

> Environmental issues have become a far more prominent 'subject' since the early international reviews. They are no longer the domain of radical youth or ecology organisations, but a central focus of political and educational debate. This needs to be reflected in future reviews.

The role of diaspora

The 'second seven' international youth policy reviews relate to at least three countries where the national diaspora is well-known: Malta, Cyprus and Armenia. It might be argued that Lithuania should also be included, but the significant Lithuanian diaspora is not discussed in the same way. What is not well-known, however, is how the diasporic influence diffuses, in both directions, in relation to young people. It was clear, for example, that young Armenians may find the chance to study abroad through family links in places such as the USA. The existence of the Armenian diaspora has assisted successive waves of emigration from Armenia (IR p. 47). The Cyprus NR (p. 173) sets out the core purpose of the Republic of Cyprus Government's Service for Overseas Cypriots:

> To ensure continuous and close contact with Overseas Cypriots and the preservation of their national identity, religion and cultural heritage, to maintain their love and interest in Cyprus and to assist with their problems and needs.

For the Armenians, it has been for the diaspora to assist with the problems and needs 'back home' – it provides over 1 billion dollars a year in support of 'day-to-day' living (remittances to relatives) as well as capital investment (IR p. 7). The bond between the 3 million Armenians in Armenia and the 6 million elsewhere in the world is sustained through many personal, financial and organisational links (draft NR p. 152). Such connections were not explored in the review of Malta (IR p. 12), though it does acknowledge the 'importance' of the "transfers in human and social capital that take place between Malta and its emigrant communities in such places as Australia, Canada, the United States of America and the United Kingdom".

> It may be less relevant in many countries, but within some countries the 'place' of its diaspora – in mythology, culture, religion, identity, economy and education – and its contribution to the lives of young people may merit very significant attention.

e. Foundation stones for effective youth policy

The first synthesis report suggested that there were three planks for the development and implementation of effective youth policy: youth research, professional training and the dissemination of good practice. This contention is largely supported by the more recent reviews, though there are some additional substantive observations emerging from them that are worth considering.

Research

Many of the international reviews appear to have suffered from an absence, or a partial absence, of research data. It is sometimes difficult to know whether such data are actually available – but were not made available – or whether they simply do not exist:

There is no hiding from the fact that statistical information in Malta is lacking and that co-ordination between relevant domains is not as healthy as one would wish it to be. (Malta IR p. 77)

The Malta international report goes on to say that the 'lines of communication' between research and policy makers need to be improved. That presupposes, of course, that the research has something to say – in other words, it has some policy relevance. Concern had been expressed, for example, in Norway (IR p. 87) that it was rather thin on policy-related and evaluation youth studies, despite its long tradition and high reputation in more academic and theoretical youth research.

Slovakia (NR p. 19) notes that it has "never had an independent institute dedicated solely to youth research" but argues (NR p. 143) that "youth research plays an important support role in the youth policy". The international report on Armenia proposes the establishment of a small youth research unit similar to that which exists currently in Slovenia (see IR pp. 51-52).

> The relationship between youth research and youth policy-making is a complex one. Youth research may be too theoretical and lack application. There may be an absence of empirical research data. The data may exist but in an unhelpful form. The data may be in an appropriate form but convey an inappropriate (political) message. The international reviews should strengthen their analysis of these relationships and responses.

Training

The Slovakia NR (pp. 143-44) says that the preparation of youth workers is a necessary precondition of youth policy implementation. The Malta IR (p. 73) discusses the professional training of youth and community workers. Training is on the agenda, but little is said about the more detailed, and difficult, questions concerning who should be trained, how, where, why, what in and what for? These are classical questions around need, curriculum and occupations. The Slovakia IR (p. 48) usefully classifies those who work with young people as:

- professionals;
- para-professionals;
- pseudo-professionals;
- volunteers.

This raises a host of further questions about what kinds of skills are required for different kinds of youth policy interventions, as well as a country's financial capacity to support appropriate professional developments. To speak generically of 'youth workers' conceals the need for specialist knowledge and skills in areas such as communications, counselling, health information and, for instance, youth justice (of which, incidentally, there are no specialist practitioners in Malta or Armenia).

> There needs to be a deeper, more refined, exploration of training provision and needs in relation to the expressed or aspirational youth policy framework in different countries.

Dissemination of good practice

We have learned very little about the methods and mechanisms by which 'good practice' is shared, critically reflected upon and perhaps more widely applied. The Cyprus IR (p. 69) alludes to various projects doing some excellent work operating in 'splendid isolation' – with apparently little opportunity to discuss their practice with a wider audience.

There are, of course, many forms for such dissemination – such as conferences, professional working groups, magazines and journals, websites and promotional documents. The 'best practice' identified in international youth policy reviews is disseminated at national level at the national hearing and internationally through presentation to the Joint Council of the Youth Directorate. It is therefore somewhat ironic that the reviews seem to have been unable to discover what might be called 'dissemination practice' in the countries concerned!

> Future international reviews should endeavour to document the variety of ways in which the best youth work delivery is communicated to others working to similar objectives.

Section 2: The international review process – reflections and recommendations

My late father was in the Royal Corps of Signals during the war. After a generally dismal time in North Africa he was stationed in places such as Florence and Prato where his job was to restore the communications systems. This meant working with local people on the ground. He made friends with them and, along with others in his unit, got invited to weddings and such like. Unlike some people of the same generation, the experience of reconstruction made a European of him. In a way I think that is what we are doing, really: putting up the telephone wires and having a drink and a meal with the local people.

(Respondent, slightly amended, with permission)

For the seven international reviews, there have been some 27 individuals involved beyond the secretariat of the Directorate of Youth and Sport. The number is imprecise, for some review team members played only a partial role in the process, for both personal and professional reasons. Moreover, though the team for Hungary was formally identified, it has not yet become operational and therefore its membership should be excluded, though some members have already been involved in other reviews. One can, therefore, safely assume that 25 individuals from governments, youth organisations and research institutes (and occasionally other settings) have contributed to the Council of Europe's international youth policy review process; of these, nine kindly provided a personal reflection on their experience. This was a disappointing response. Despite two requests for at least a brief note (one circulated at the beginning of January 2006, the second at the beginning of March 2006), most people did not even have the courtesy to respond at all. One member of the Advisory Council said there was nothing to say.

For the six reviews in question, there were 30 team 'slots' for individuals beyond the secretariat.[26] I was involved in three of them, leaving 27 slots. These nine responses cover 14 slots, for a number of individuals who responded had been involved in more than one review. Indeed, some had also been involved from a national perspective, and also in Council of Europe youth policy advisory missions,[27] and had some distinctive observations as a result. However, the coverage was uneven in terms of different categories of participant. There was only one response from a member of the CDEJ and only one from a member of the Advisory Council. The

---

26. Who usually provided just one member – in every case for these six reviews, Mr Peter Lauritzen – but occasionally provided an extra participant, which was the case in three of these reviews.
27. Advisory Missions to Slovenia, Croatia, and Bosnia and Herzegovina.

remaining seven responses were largely from the youth researchers who occupied seven of the 10 slots (not counting the three I occupied) that had been allocated to youth researchers, and there were also responses from two (out of five) of the 'experts' who had sometimes been included, in lieu of youth researchers, for their specialist knowledge of particular issues. In the case of one review team, I had no response at all; in contrast, I had a complete response from another one. I was rapporteur for three of the reviews; only one of the other rapporteurs did not respond.

This makes, then, for a rather fragmented and incomplete picture. Yet the accounts provided are remarkably consistent in both their praise and their criticism. I very much doubt, from my own experience as well, that additional contributions would have told a significantly different story. That 'story' addresses each step of the journey as a member of a review team and produces a range of suggestions about how both process and product might be improved.

------> ## Preliminary visit

The preliminary visit is, by definition, a part of the international review process that precedes the composition of the review team. It was established first in Lithuania (the eighth review) in order to better understand and identify the priority concerns of the country to be reviewed. This would, then, to some extent at least, inform the composition of the international team. Team members would simply learn of these priorities once they had become involved. Nevertheless, they are aware that these preliminary visits have been carried out exclusively by one individual within the Directorate of Youth and Sports, someone who was described as "very difficult to replace ... his experience, knowledge and flair are incomparable and beyond question". There were concerns about who might replace or substitute for him, leading to the recommendation that:

> Other people should be identified (within or beyond the Directorate of Youth and Sports) who might be able to alternate or follow in the role of conducting a preliminary visit to the host country in order to identify key priorities for scrutiny and debate. These individuals should accompany the individual presently responsible for this task in order to 'learn the ropes'.

------> ## Review team composition

There was some puzzlement over exactly how the international review teams were put together, despite the clear precedent concerning the types of people to be involved (one CDEJ, one Advisory Council, one Secretariat, three youth researchers,[28] one of whom to serve as rapporteur). Beyond that, however, the Secretariat endeavoured to strike a balance across a range of criteria, from gender and experience to more practical issues such as availability and interest.

By and large, it was felt that review teams had been well composed, seeking to establish a 'complementarity' between the individuals concerned. And although, sometimes, invitations to participate had come 'out of the blue', other individuals had actively sought a place in the team on account of a particular set of interests

---

28. This did change in the course of these reviews, with one youth researcher 'position' sometimes replaced with an alternative type of expert – with, for example, training experience or specific knowledge about a particular issue (such as conflict resolution or the situation of ethnic minorities).

------>

or experience. All respondents said they had been very happy to take part: they felt "honoured", "challenged", "delighted" and "excited" to have been asked.

It was acknowledged that putting together an effective team was a tricky business, which had typically been tackled very well, but there were, nevertheless, some useful further proposals. These were essentially to do with using team composition for one review as a vehicle for connecting and ensuring continuities around the wider review process. To some extent, this already happens:[29] CDEJ members who have already hosted reviews have been invited to chair a subsequent review. It is suggested, however, that:

> There should always be a connection with the previous review – either from the previous team or the 'hosting' CDEJ member for the country concerned – and a connection with the next planned review: ideally a youth researcher from that country (the nominated youth research correspondent, if there is one) who might then be expected to 'lead' on the production of its national report.

The production and timing of the national report

Ideally the timing for the production of the national report is agreed during the preliminary visit and the setting of provisional dates for the first visit of the international team. Furthermore, the content of the national report should also be agreed, though, through building on the experience of the review process, there is now something of a template supporting a reasonably consistent approach.

The national report is a critical foundation stone for enabling learning about youth policy in the host country by the international team; without it, the basis of preparation becomes something of a lottery and denies the possibility of any sort of orientation towards the task at hand.

The prevailing view was that:

> "it would not be out of place to make suggestions on what one expects to find in a national report" (such as contextual information about the host country, current policies, relevant research papers, national youth policy aspirations and developments).

Firmer prescription of desired content would simply be an incremental development of what has already taken place. The national reports have generally been of a high quality in terms of policy description, statistical presentation and more qualitative commentary. Of more concern has been their timing for, far from being completed (at least in a final draft form) prior to the first visit of the international review team, a number have not appeared in any form until after the second visit – indeed, in some cases, only just before the international hearing. This was considered to be completely unacceptable, a perversion of the original process, and – arguably – an opportunity for the host country to alter its national presentation to take account of, and possibly 'head off at the pass', the more acute criticisms made through

---

29. Having continuity through sequential participation by at least one member of the previous team was in fact one suggestion from the very first review (of Finland in 1997). Then it was argued that the rapporteur should join the next review as a youth researcher member; but this was not implemented at the time. No member of the Finland review team participated in the next review, of the Netherlands.

the international review. There was some conviction that the timing of the national report needed more regulation:

> An international review should not start before the national report is completed and published. This report is the main tool by which the review team can focus on, and start to understand, the host country's situation, perceptions, expectations and needs which, at least for programme and agenda purposes (see below), should not be re-written for the duration of the international review process.

Preparation for the international review

There was considerable criticism about the quality and nature of preparation for participating in the international reviews. Some alleged there was a complete absence of any preparation. Others described receiving a 'scary overload' of material, feeling under some pressure to read it all. There were members of teams who took it upon themselves to activate a learning curve on the country concerned. Some team members waited for information or instruction that never came. Many described a state of confusion and uncertainty following their invitation to participate: what exactly was involved, what was their role and responsibility in the process? There was, however, a general 'sensitisation' effect, following invitation, in relation to the country concerned. Quite a lot was learned from news items, media reports and wider discussion.

Various suggestions were made to rectify the state of confusion that also produced considerable frustration. (It was, of course, made much worse in relation to those reviews where there was no national report available.) Generally it was felt that an opening team meeting on arrival for the first visit was not sufficient; it was often too rushed and left too much to chance:

> There needs to be a more robust approach to preparing the international review team for its task. This could take the form of a preliminary team meeting, after receipt and reading of the national report and prior to the first visit. Though the programme for the first visit might have been agreed on the occasion of the preliminary visit, this preliminary team meeting would enable members to meet each other (not all would already know each other), discuss divisions of labour and agree working methods, and consider prospective agenda items within the meetings scheduled for the first visit.
>
> Alternatively, it was suggested that a training and briefing pack should be made available to all new participants in the review process, outlining its history and its elements, and indicating expectations and responsibilities.
>
> A third proposal was that, beyond the information provided in the national report, the Youth Directorate should identify its contacts within the host country and notify the international team; this would or could provide an additional strand to information-gathering.

Members of international review teams, with the exception of the rapporteur, are not paid for their contribution. They do, however, now[30] receive a per diem at the standard Council of Europe rate. This is never intended to substitute for any

---

30. Initially, only receipted travel expenses were covered.

payment – it covers accommodation (50%), meals (30%) and incidental expenses (20%). Whether it in fact covers an individual's costs during an international review depends on the country concerned and the extent to which the host country extends hospitality, especially in terms of evening meals. Theoretically, in a 'cheap' country that provided very generous hospitality, it might be possible to make money from the per diem. In practice, the per diem usually does cover genuine daily costs, but travel reimbursement rarely covers the real transportation costs that have been incurred, because of the administrative rules of the Council of Europe. This is a huge bone of contention, both within and beyond the international reviews, but it is especially contentious amongst review team members in view of the time sacrifice demanded, the effort invested and the fact that no formal payment is made for this contribution. The risk of being left out of pocket (a small risk but nonetheless a real one) has proved an irritant to some of those who have been involved and apparently a deterrent to others from participating at all.

> It is important that, in the round, review team members are not left out of pocket. 'In the round' means that all legitimately receipted expenses for travel and subsistence costs incurred during a review are fully covered by the combination of per diem allowances and travel reimbursements. This is an absolutely minimum requirement.

Team relationships

Interpersonal relationships across review teams were typically described as "very positive" and "excellent", though sometimes it was noted that this did not always translate into effective professional relationships and sometimes, perhaps fortunately, compensated for them. Respondents wrote of the time it took to "get used to" the working methods of the team and to "work out" their professional position and potential contribution within it.

Participation in the team was considered to be, simultaneously, "demanding" and "tiring", and "enriching" and "enjoyable". The recurrent experience, however, was that it was "frustrating", largely because of a lack of clarity about individual roles. Those completely new to the process either felt lost or settled passively into an 'apprenticeship' role; in both cases, though, they quietly resented the 'perceived hierarchies' based on (in)experience and (un)familiarity. Invariably they would have welcomed a much fuller explanation and exploration of who was expected to do what (and why). As the review process unfolded, most members felt that their contribution was valued, but the 'disorientation' of their early days was not forgotten.

Some teams spent virtually all their waking hours together, taking every opportunity – beyond the formal programme – to discuss developments in the review as well as other issues of common interest. Other teams spent far less time together, with individual members slipping off quite regularly to see personal friends, to attend other commitments, or just to relax alone. There are, of course, no golden rules on these matters; the concern expressed was that different team members often had different ideas about what was appropriate, producing irritation when others did not conform to this:

> A clearer sense of minimum 'requirements' – perhaps agreed by the whole team during a preliminary meeting – concerning attendance during the formal

programme and during more social occasions would establish greater clarity for team members as to what is expected of them.

During each visit, based on team discussion and agreement, different team members should perhaps take the lead role in shaping and guiding the agenda within particular meetings during the formal programme.

At the conclusion of the second visit (or possibly at the very end of the process), the international review team should reflect on and evaluate how effectively it had worked as a team.

Visiting the host country: hosting and hospitality

All but one of the reviews involved two visits by the international team to the host country. These were usually each about a week long (four or five working days), with some three months in between them. The first visit typically consisted of a programme of meetings in the capital city, usually with various government ministries and national organisations. This programme was normally arranged by the host country following some discussion during the preliminary meeting with the Council of Europe secretariat. The second visit was more concerned with regional and local delivery of youth policy. It was desirable for the international team to spend much of its time away from the capital city and centre of administration. The programme for this second visit was usually more proactively negotiated by the international team, to ensure contact with groups or around issues that appeared to need more scrutiny. Sometimes the overall programme (both visits) was 'topped and tailed', at the start by a high-level introductory, scene-setting meeting, and at the finish by a similar meeting to test tentative findings and conclusions. In between the two visits, the international team had the opportunity to develop and consolidate its knowledge and perspectives.

Rarely, however, did all these features fall into place at the planned time in the process. This was sometimes the 'fault' of the Council of Europe and sometimes of the host country. Most elements, nevertheless, tended to feature at some point in the two visits, though their sequence was sometimes less than desirable.

There was a range of observations about the shape, balance and 'penetration' of the programme during visits,[31] and the role of hosting and hospitality. The accounts were very mixed. Objective descriptions were clearly accurate when there were allegations that the programme was "too crowded" or that the international team had been "abandoned" or, conversely, "smothered" by hospitality. The questions lay in the interpretation of these approaches to the international review. Some suggested there was little professional interest in the review per se; it was more about a symbolic political value. Others worried that the programme was intentionally 'packed' by the host country to prevent the international team having any chance to meet dissenting voices.[32] It was also mooted that too much observation of protocol and diplomacy paralysed the international team from

---

31. In the text of the Malta IR (p. 44) it is noted: "On first appearances Malta seems to be a reasonably homogenous society in terms of ethnicity, culture and religion. Nevertheless, minorities do exist within Maltese society. Unfortunately the review team did not have the opportunity to meet any members of the minority communities. In the circumstances it is therefore difficult to comment authoritatively on the way in which the society deals with such groups as minority ethnic communities, asylum seekers, and gays and lesbians."

32. One respondent wrote: "The representativeness of the people one is meeting is an issue that nags most Review Teams, I imagine."

asking incisive questions, leaving it with a very selective (selected) and superficial picture. Diplomatic requirements also meant that, in some cases, critical issues (either of substance, or concerning non-compliance with procedures) were left unspoken.

Despite these concerns, and despite the fact that team members had often had quite mixed experiences,[33] most expressed great appreciation for the often quite lavish hospitality bestowed on them. They acknowledged the difficulties attached to striking a suitable balance between a formal work programme, time for discussion, the need for some relaxation, the possibility of some social (touristic) entertainment, and perhaps the pressure for some more formal 'ceremonial' engagement. After all, for some countries, the visit was a very significant occasion (even if some thought the team was from the European Commission!).

A serious problem was the lack of time for reflection and planning by the international team, and whether or not someone from the host country should be present when this did take place. Again, this is not a plea for prescription but a statement that the issue needs attention. Reflection and planning time can be both more formal (for example, a half-hour session each day immediately after breakfast and again after lunch), and less formal (for example, over a meal in the evening). Whether or not someone from the host country should be present is debatable and dependent on what the issues are. They can be very helpful to field and clarify questions, but they may also inhibit a full and frank discussion for reasons of protocol and diplomacy (and the wish to avoid seeming insulting to their efforts). There is usually a sound case for some 'critical complicity' between the review team and the hosting group; after all, both are, even if in different ways, committed to the development of youth policy. That is a prima facie reason for having a hosting presence at reflection and planning meetings – for clarification, guidance and advice. But there may be times when this is undesirable. The review team needs to have a strategy for addressing such issues.

There was wholehearted support for the 'ideal' framework for the review process – the first visit to the central administration, a period for exchange and consolidation, then a second visit to address emergent themes and more operational issues in the regions.

All reviews should involve at least two visits: even small countries have complex histories and challenging issues with which to grapple.

The shape and balance of the programme needs careful attention and considered negotiation between hosting groups and the international team (or its nominated lead).

In particular, space must be set aside, and defended, for the international team to be able to reflect on how its work is progressing and to plan properly for meetings that lie ahead.

With one exception, it was reported that there was very little exchange of information between members of review teams in between visits. Indeed, it was also noted that there was hardly any communication between review team members and those

33. One particular frustration, in relation to some reviews, was the amount of time consumed with translation and interpretation, and simply getting it organised in the first place!

from the hosting group (usually government civil servants), despite promises to keep in touch and to send on various items of information.

> There may be different reasons for maintaining contact between visits, but there is unlikely to be a good reason for not doing so at all. Simply sharing emergent information on the host country, stumbled upon by one individual or another, would be a 'bottom line'; a 'top line' would be the draft preparation by different team members of elements of the international report. Once more, the key point is that this should not be left to chance or in a vacuum, but purposefully debated.

The production of the international report

The four international reports I have written have been described, in some quarters, as 'dense'. I hope this does not mean 'thick' (as in stupid!); I think it means that they have the privileged intensity of a native English speaker, which may make it rather hard for other potential collaborators (i.e. other members of a team) to 'intrude'. A rapporteur for an earlier international review accused me of writing too much, which may be true. Some rapporteurs, however, have been criticised for writing too little.

There are, therefore, some key questions about the format and length of the international report, and the process by which it is put together. Ultimately, it is the responsibility of the rapporteur, but it is not, or should not be, their sole responsibility. International reports have been composed in very different ways. At one end of the spectrum is one report that "went through a number of drafts, which were circulated to colleagues and all of them made useful written comments". At the other is one where there was "little or no active involvement of the team in drafting the text of the report". One respondent said that proactive and feedback communication from team members other than the rapporteur should not be contingent on volunteering or promises, but a requirement of participation, to be brokered and monitored through the secretariat.

The issue does demand further debate. Team members recognise that rapporteurs carry the lead responsibility in producing the international report (for which they are paid), but team members also need to recognise that the compilation of the international report is a shared and open process, not a closed one.[34] Some did not feel this. One, who had promised to make a contribution but did not, wrote that

> the area that I have found most difficult to define in my role – and where I have not been very proactive in seeking it out – is in my relation to the overall report process beyond the visits. ... After the second visit, I was not clear how I could contribute.

Another respondent rather critically alleged that there was too much power in the hands of the rapporteur, and that "non-reporters" were in a "secondary role".

There was also an issue about dissenting voices within the review team. This had been a matter of significance in an earlier review, where one member did not wish to be associated with the final international report. Within the six reviews being considered here, there was one in which one team member wished to register a stronger perspective; this was accommodated within the international report with the full consent of all the other team members.

---

34. After all, the international report is collectively authored by all members of the international review team.

The job of the rapporteur is acknowledged to be a rather lonely one. It was suggested that new rapporteurs might have on-line mentors from amongst those who have done the job previously.

Returning to the question of format and length, there was general appreciation of the earlier synthesis report (Williamson 2002), which did promote a particular framework for considering themes and issues in national youth policy. It was suggested that this framework, or template, might be refined, perhaps with the addition of quality standards relating to the international review process itself. There was certainly a view that there could and should be a uniformity in the structure of the international reports, one which need not repeat material that (ideally) should be contained within the host country's national report.

> If team members are to play a part in contributing to, or responding to, drafts of the international report, then this does need to be formalised in some way – possibly through some system of rewards or sanctions. Too often, material has been promised and never delivered. Too often, feedback has been requested, and never given. This places the rapporteur in an invidious position, especially where deadlines or hearing are looming.
>
> Minority positions and perspectives within the international team obviously jeopardise the 'integrity' of the final international report, but there is now a model for accommodating them while retaining an overall consensual report.
>
> New rapporteurs may benefit from having the opportunity to access advice, guidance and support from those who have previously fulfilled this role.
>
> There is a strong case for the standardisation of international reports, using an agreed template (building on the existing synthesis report and adding quality standards concerning the process) and avoiding the duplication of material that should be in a national report.

----> The national and international hearings

Since the eighth international review (of Lithuania), there has been not only an international hearing (the presentation of the international report to the Joint Council of the CDEJ and the Advisory Council, the statutory organs that set the agenda for the Youth Directorate through co-management) but also a national hearing. The latter is designed to be an open meeting in the host country's capital in order to present and debate the draft international report. Points can be clarified and corrections can be made prior to finalising the international report for the international hearing.

There was a view that the national hearings are constructed across a continuum from tokenism, through interest, to commitment. There were also questions about how well publicised such hearings are; in one, not even all those who had contributed to the review process were always aware that the hearing was taking place. It was felt that publicity and seriousness went together: where the intention was for a rather staged, public relations event, it was suggested that those attending were more likely to have been selected, vetted and invited. Where there was more commitment to advancing the youth policy agenda through serious debate, it was more likely that an 'open door' approach to the hearing would have been established. Few would dispute that the standard of the national hearings have been, as one person put it, "of mixed quality".

An ironic twist arising from the implementation of a national hearing is that it permits the host country to have advance warning of areas where the international report is likely to criticise its youth policy. This permits the host country to prepare a pre-emptive strike for the international hearing, for representatives of the host country government (often the relevant minister) speak first.[35] Indeed, at one hearing, the 'introductory' contributions from the host country lasted so long they left little time for the international report to be presented.

> It is imperative that the time allocations between different presenters at both the national and international hearings are fairly allocated and properly enforced, to ensure parity of opportunity and intervention.

Follow-up

One rationale for the national hearing is to permit all actors in the youth policy context to have the opportunity to hear a constructive critique of that policy, to consider what kinds of responses might be possible and appropriate, and to hear of any commitments that the government might make. While it would be absurd to think that national administrations would take on board even all those issues raised by the international team considered by the host country to be valid, it is hoped that some key concerns would, over time, be accorded political and professional attention.

There is a view that commitment to some follow-up activity and some monitoring of this by the Council of Europe should be an additional, and stronger, part of the overall process. Respondents had little evidence of follow-up activity; and where they were aware of some, it had been limited and poorly executed.

> Where commitments are made to following through issues raised in the international report, there should be a more formalised approach to reviewing and discussing subsequent policy development – perhaps after two years.

Conclusion – the future of the international reviews

> I believe the impact of the combination of the national and international reports has a great potential both on the national and the European youth policy dimensions, but then again it depends on the follow-up to these reports how the situation for young people in the country can improve. For this, true political commitment is needed and not only the prestige of having had the international peer review done. (Respondent)

No-one has suggested to me, either verbally or in writing, that the process of international reviews of national youth policy, established by the Youth Directorate of the Council of Europe in 1997, should be abandoned. Virtually everyone has said that they should be improved, building on a platform which itself has been a site of continuous improvement over time.

---

35. This is also a key reason for requiring the production and publication of the national report before the start of an international review (see above); otherwise a double pre-emptive strike is possible, for a 'last minute' national report can ensure that its presentation addresses the criticisms of the international report, thus somewhat undermining the credibility of the latter.

There will always be questions about the value of the approach to the host countries involved. Some, undoubtedly, will volunteer for the process for symbolic rather than serious purposes. Some might question the value of the reviews to the Council of Europe in formulating a youth policy framework with some pertinence to all of its member countries. This would be a harder criticism to sustain, for the review process has made a significant contribution both to the concept of 'youth policy' in Europe and to the dissemination of operational activity across a range of youth policy themes from one part of Europe to another.

All commentators testified to the value of the process. Ultimately the process and the product are the result of a delicate balance between political, diplomatic, personal and professional (academic) concerns, which generally have been managed admirably by the secretariat from the Youth Directorate. Youth researchers themselves do not have to juggle such responsibilities. Their constant anxiety, as one individual put it, is whether they are genuinely acting as a 'stranger in a strange land', producing acute observations on important issues that otherwise might be missed. Or are they just 'stupid foreigners', raising issues that are quite irrelevant, meaningless and useless for the country concerned. This is an inevitable anxiety for the international review teams as a whole; after all, they have very little time to become acquainted with the always complex historical and political culture of the host country as well as its approaches to meeting the needs of its young people.

The first seven youth policy reviews were something of a potpourri of approaches, with very few common reference points and little consistency in approach. The next six, which have been the focus of this reflection, have certainly been more uniform in many ways, but those who have been involved have produced a series of recommendations that may strengthen and systematise a valued process still further.

Section 3: A brief comment on benchmarks

At one point in the Lithuania international report, its education system is judged against 'European standards'. From the other end, the Armenia draft national report frequently talks of working towards "international standards". This begs a host of questions concerning (a) what these standards are and (b) whether or not it is appropriate for emergent European and other developing countries to be 'judged' against them.

The 2002 synthesis report proposed that national youth policies might be considered in relation to five Cs, which have since become known as the 'components' of youth policy: coverage, capacity, competence, co-ordination and cost. It also suggested that there should be some reflection on four (or eight) Ds, or the circular creative or obstructive 'dynamics' of youth policy: political Drive, decentralisation, Delivery, difficulties, Debate, dissent, Development, direction, and back to Drive.

These Cs and Ds were nothing more than tentative ideas, though they have achieved some currency and have been taken up in some quarters in the debate on youth policy (and ignored or rejected in others!). They are, of course, not the only measures and they are certainly not official markers. A more official framework for deliberation and judgment, produced a year after the publication of the first synthesis report, is the youth policy indicators established by the Council of Europe.[36] These are described and discussed in some detail in the Malta IR (pp. 16-19). There are also some rather more straightforward 'tests' of the potential efficacy of youth policy, such as Peter Lauritzen's 'checklist',[37] which includes factors such as budget, legislation, the existence of a national youth council, and relevant structures for management and delivery.

There are plenty of crossovers between these different models but, as the Council of Europe's review process expands beyond the heart of central and western Europe, much of their content seems less and less significant – or at least rather less important than other things. In those contexts, international reports may need to take more cognisance of frameworks such as the UN World Programme of Action for Youth, and indeed, the UN's Millennium Development Goals.[38] Equally, there may also be a case of looking more specifically at targets and frameworks in

---

36. See Expert Group on Youth Policy Indicators (2003), *Final Report*, Strasbourg: Council of Europe Youth Directorate.

37. Peter Lauritzen, Head of Youth in the Council of Europe's Directorate of Youth and Sport – he formulated this relatively simple checklist ahead of an 'advisory mission' to Slovenia in 2002.

38. Julie Larsen, from the Focal Point on Youth at the United Nations, has prepared a very useful chart showing the 'linkages' between these two UN initiatives: the 15 priority areas of the WPAY and the eight goals and 18 targets of the MDGs.

discrete policy areas. For example, in health, there is the WHO European Region "Health for All Targets",[39] mentioned in the national report for Malta (p. 74) as the guiding influence on youth health policy in Malta. And, at a national level, there are very likely to be target and benchmarks set for many areas of 'youth policy' which, again, international teams may wish to probe more deeply.

39. WHO Regional Office for Europe: European Health for All database, http://www.who.dk.hfa.

Conclusion

Both the national reports and the international review process itself need to be considered from three angles: in the words of Karen Evans (2005), what is "espoused, enacted and experienced". The Lithuania NR (p. 8) acknowledges from the start the "gap between good intentions and scope of realised actions". What is written in national reports may bear little relation to practice on the ground, and this may also be the case with international review reports, though these have become more firmly grounded and consistent since the framework produced by the first synthesis report (Williamson 2002).

There will, of course, always be a range of challenges in relation both to substantive presentations and administrative processes. It will always be a case of seeking to balance consistency (and thereby the prospect of comparability) with diversity (which thereby acknowledges the distinctive needs and priorities of different countries).

Beyond the indicative recommendations raised throughout this synthesis, there remain a number of overarching questions:

- How should the national report be composed – in terms of the amount of theory, the structure, the style? To what extent should a range of de facto academic essays or reports 'lifted' from other places, with considerable peripheral data (which is certainly the impression given by the Malta NR), be an acceptable product?

- Who should compose the national report? Various approaches have been used over the course of all 13 reviews: the presentation of different perspectives (the first review of Finland); outsourcing and subcontracting to a university (Cyprus), a nominated team of experts (Armenia), a huge team of contributors co-ordinated by the government (Slovakia). Should there be a more coherent model?

- Ultimately, who is the national report for? Or is it produced for a number of different purposes and audiences, just one of which is the Council of Europe international review? If, however, it is primarily or exclusively for the international review, should not the Council of Europe have more say in its content, style and contribution?

- What is the capacity of a country to put together and publish – to 'blueprint' expectations and timescales – the national report?

- Should there be greater consistency in the terminology used in both national and international reports: substance misuse rather than abuse; abortion rather than artificial interruption of pregnancy?

- Should follow-up plans be required and subjected to monitoring, consultation and review?

There are, of course, similar questions about the construction and format of international reports:

- the credibility of source material drawn from elsewhere and dependency on a restricted number of external reports (the Lithuania IR draws disproportionately on the UN Development Report 2001);

- the extent to which researchers' (usually the rapporteur's) own perspectives should encroach on commentary and analysis;

- the balance between substantiated (referenced) evidence and more discursive assertion drawn from observation or individual comment;

- ensuring feedback prior to national hearings and making the necessary corrections to ensure accuracy and sustain the credibility of the international report.[40]

In spite of all these caveats, final questions and notes of caution, there can be no doubt about the value of the 'stranger's eye'. Though all international review teams have to embark on a quite dramatic learning curve, embracing the challenge of a new culture and context, they have generally done so with professionalism and efficiency, impressing their hosts with the speed with which they have acquired knowledge and understanding of the youth policy framework and the key issues within it. Of course, there have been moments when members of international teams have been 'chasing phantoms' (issues that are either not present or not relevant), but for the most part legitimate concerns have been pursued and addressed. Host governments and organisations generally speak well of the international review process in sharpening their attention to key issues and stimulating consideration of new ideas.

The international review model is therefore, by and large, a good one. But of course there is room for improvement in both the process and the product. Such improvement can be achieved in particular by the following:

- clearer understanding and co-operation by the host country, especially on timely delivery of the national report and the organisation of the international visit;

- careful composition of the international review team and more robust preparation of the team, including ensuring clear understanding of the expectations and prospective contribution of individual team members.

Beyond these essential prerequisites for successful individual country reviews, consideration should be given to two further issues that would consolidate the international review process and provide value-added comparative analysis:

- sequentially: a follow-up, perhaps two years later, on the general reception to and action flowing from the review, and/or on specific critical concerns;

---

40. The Lithuania IR (p. 47) refers to the Ministry for Labour and Social Protection. This is inaccurate; it was the Ministry for Labour and Social Security.

- thematically: learning through comparing the distinct approaches of different countries on specific youth policy themes, such as health policy or vocational training. This would permit the production of 'key issue and good practice' reports, enabling other countries to reflect on their own policy and practice in these areas – and thus better fulfilling one of the core objectives of the international review process.

The reason for producing this report is to contribute to the continuous improvement of the international review process in order to better achieve all three core objectives (outlined in the Introduction). It is to be hoped that this discussion will support improvements in the framework, the process and the product.

Appendix 1: Recommendations

Section 1: Building on the 2002 framework

a. Concepts of 'youth' and 'youth policy'

1. There needs to be a place in national reports to describe and comment on the 'lived experiences' of different segments/sections of young people. The life and prospects of a university student in the capital are going to be very different from the young farm labourer in the countryside. Some case studies of 'my life' were requested during the Armenia review, but none was provided.

2. There is, then, a new debate to be had about the separation and integration of 'youth' issues in relation to questions of childhood and family life.

3. A critically reflective analysis of the social condition of young people – a 'youth sociology' – should be strengthened as a component of national reports.

4. More explicit consideration should be given to the duration of contemporary phases of youth policy development in different countries, especially for both comparative purposes and in relation to a proposed 'follow-up' element in the international review process.

5. The evolution of national youth policy should be a stronger component of national reports, identifying distinct developmental phases and the reasons for them.

6. Both national and international reports need to pay attention to how 'youth policy' relates to the 'pathway' between tradition and change, and its position between affirmatory and anticipatory culture.

b. Structure and infrastructure

7. We should perhaps not get too sidetracked by the assumption that youth policy will remain incoherent and slow in development in the absence of

formal legislation. What demands critical evaluation is the strength of the mechanisms in place, be they legal or administrative.

8. Future international reviews need to explore more closely the nature of relationships between youth organisations, their national youth council and their government. Questions of independence and an authentic place in civil society are always a matter for debate and of perspective, but too much often seems to be taken for granted.

9. Making sense of the overall budget is one challenge for international reviews. Understanding how it is allocated – organisationally, geographically, on issues, and at what levels – is immensely complex. Yet documenting the absolute and relative allocations to young people in different countries is a challenge to which future international reviews must rise.

10. Where national youth agencies at arm's length from government do exist, future reviews need to establish more clearly their roles, responsibilities and functions. What is the level and nature of their independence? How broad and deep are their responsibilities? To what extent does government exercise an influence over the strategic direction and content of their work?

11. Ombudspersons have tended to be associated with children and, as a result, perhaps somewhat overlooked when considering the position of young people. Yet they have the potential to play a key role in the protection of human rights and extension of opportunities for young people, and need more thorough attention within the review process.

12. The first synthesis report suggested that part of the framework of youth policy was 'structures for delivery', both vertical and horizontal, and taking account of the role of youth organisations. This report suggests that greater attention needs to be paid to the organisation of 'delivery relationships' – how is youth policy taken forward and who is included within (and excluded from) the processes of decision-making as implementation shifts from central planning to local delivery.

c. Policy domains

13. In addressing educational issues, international reviews need to ensure (1) a close focus on (a) structure and organisation, (b) content, (c) delivery, and (d) standards. They also need to give attention to (2) drop-out, inclusion and achievement. Finally, they need to unravel (3) the real understanding and practice of the concept of non-formal education.

14. Training and employment – once a clear alternative for young people who ceased to be engaged in education – has now become muddled, muddied and mixed with other activity, as young people opt, or are forced, to create

their own individualised version of 'sliced life'. More hidden economic activity is likely to be taking place, both in the labour market and in the domestic arena. Future international reviews will need to explore these complexities more carefully.

15. Concerns about illegal drug use should not overshadow wider, and usually more prevalent, health concerns. Beyond prevalence issues, there is also the need to focus on the range of dedicated youth health services available and the extent to which young people are aware of, and make use of them.

16. The place of religion in the contemporary lives of young people – whether as the basis for values or as the mechanism for social and community integration – has perhaps been underestimated. Future reviews should give it greater attention.

17. Future international reviews need to be conscious of (a) the use of leisure time for both traditional and modern culture, (b) issues concerning unequal access to leisure time activities, and (c) the contraction of leisure time in the interests of enhancing formal learning and qualification.

18. Military service remains a significant feature in young people's lives in some countries, though with different meanings and risks. It is, equally, a significant feature of 'youth policy' in some countries, though again within different priorities and with different objectives. The nature of alternative service possibilities reflects the different political contexts in which it is available. This synthesis report confirms its place within the repertoire of youth policy initiatives: as the Armenia draft NR (p. 138) notes, the army is the biggest youth organisation in Armenia and commands the greatest level of trust amongst young people.

19. Future international reviews need to pay more attention to the family context and family policy. This is imperative given the overwhelming general evidence about extended youth transitions and greater sustained 'attachment' to families of origin. It is also important given the increasingly migratory working habits of young adults in relation to both families of origin and destination. And the 'sanctity' of family life and responsibility has to be reflected upon in terms of how this may inhibit important policy activity both within the family and beyond it in other policy domains.

20. The international review process has a key role in gathering robust data on housing issues affecting young people. These concern the housing status of young people, their aspirations, access to affordable independent living, and mechanisms for supporting housing transitions.

21. Future international reviews should map the changing profile of youth offending and consider the coherence of youth justice responses in relation to wider youth policy, as well as exploring the range of interventions available for the character and severity of that offending profile.

d. Cross-cutting issues

22. Youth participation and citizenship may be a fundamental cross-cutting theme but it remains a challenge across the spectrum of possible 'facilitating' contexts and activities; it is at different stages in different countries, and it can mean very different things. The important point for the international reviews is to document the repertoire of opportunities, experiences and initiatives that are considered to assist these outcomes.

23. Rather than dwell on academic definitions of 'exclusion' (which will be endless) or seek to pinpoint specific excluded groups of young people, the 'social inclusion' focus of the international reviews should be on public strategies for access and inclusion. Reviews should reflect on their efficacy from both an international and subjective perspective.

24. This synthesis report confirms the need to explore youth information through both the services available and the ways in which they are (or are not) used by young people.

25. Future international reviews need not only distil the specific complexities of multiculturalism within the particular country under review but also endeavour to make contact with less visible 'minority' groups of young people to explore their experiences.

26. Mobility and internationalism are, self-evidently, more than studying abroad and InterRailing. Their complexity needs to be unravelled during international reviews, especially in terms of education and employment, coerced migration, whether or not people return or stay, and access to and barriers concerning European programmes.

27. There is plenty of lip service to equal opportunities. International reviews need to explore beyond issues of gender equality and consider the position of young people with disabilities and different sexual orientation who have, to date, been given insufficient explicit attention in the process.

28. Though discussion remains sparse, it is likely that future reviews will need to give greater attention both to the resurgence of old forms of racism and extremism and new forms of radicalism and fundamentalism.

29. The 'glocal' mantra favoured by youth cultural theorists and internationalists may conceal much sharper tensions, even conflicts, between sustaining local tradition and embracing global influences. How this is managed

and experienced in the lives of young people may be a useful focus for the international policy reviews.

30. Given the critical impact of new technologies both in the lives of young people and in the framework for the delivery of youth policy, they merit considerably more analysis in future reports than they have received in the past.

31. The international reviews have tended to focus on national and then local youth issues, arguably to the neglect of regional questions. More exploration and debate are required about relationships between the centre and the periphery, especially with regard to regional (youth) strategies concerned with issues such as migration, information, leisure and culture, as well as key infrastructure dimensions such as education, employment and housing.

32. The pace of 'urbanisation' of most societies is unlikely to slow down but it does have huge implications for the sustainability of rural communities – their economies, leisure infrastructure and demographic balance in particular. Young people have a central place in these trends – they are more likely to leave but, conversely, it will be their enterprise that will revive the countryside. This has been a somewhat neglected discussion in the international reviews to date.

33. Youth policy development is not immune from the normal evolution of political bureaucracy, whereby early 'insiders' consolidate their positions and, in time, form a privileged elite at the expense of latecomers and outsiders. Robust scrutiny of such situations would seem to be an important role for the international reviews.

34. Environmental issues have become a far more prominent 'subject' since the early international reviews. They are no longer the domain of radical youth or ecology organisations, but a central focus of political and educational debate. This needs to be reflected in future reviews.

35. It may be less relevant in many countries, but within some countries the 'place' of its diaspora – in mythology, culture, religion, identity, economy and education – and its contribution to the lives of young people may merit very significant attention.

e. Foundation stones for effective youth policy

36. The relationship between youth research and youth policy-making is a complex one. Youth research may be too theoretical and lack application. There may be an absence of empirical research data. The data may exist but in an unhelpful form. The data may be in an appropriate form but convey an inappropriate (political) message. The international reviews should strengthen their analysis of these relationships and responses.

37. There needs to be a deeper, more refined, exploration of training provision and needs in relation to the expressed or aspirational youth policy framework in different countries.

38. Future international reviews should endeavour to document the variety of ways in which the best youth work delivery is communicated to others working to similar objectives.

Section 2: The international review process — reflections and recommendations

39. Other people should be identified (within or beyond the Directorate of Youth and Sports) who might be able to alternate or follow in the role of conducting a preliminary visit to the host country in order to identify key priorities for scrutiny and debate. These individuals should accompany the individual presently responsible for this task in order to 'learn the ropes'.

40. There should always be a connection with the previous review – either from the previous team or the 'hosting' CDEJ member for the country concerned – and a connection with the next planned review: ideally a youth researcher from that country (the nominated youth research correspondent, if there is one) who might then be expected to 'lead' on the production of its national report.

41. "It would not be out of place to make suggestions on what one expects to find in a national report" (such as contextual information about the host country, current policies, relevant research papers, national youth policy aspirations and developments).

42. An international review should not start before the national report is completed and published. This report is the main tool by which the review team can focus on, and start to understand, the host country's situation, perceptions, expectations and needs which, at least for programme and agenda purposes (see below), should not be re-written for the duration of the international review process.

43. There needs to be a more robust approach to preparing the international review team for its task. This could take the form of a preliminary team meeting, after receipt and reading of the national report and prior to the first visit. Though the programme for the first visit might have been agreed on the occasion of the preliminary visit, this preliminary team meeting would enable members to meet each other (not all would already know each other), discuss divisions of labour and agree working methods, and consider prospective agenda items within the meetings scheduled for the first visit.

Alternatively, it was suggested that a training and briefing pack should be made available to all new participants in the review process, outlining its history and its elements, and indicating expectations and responsibilities.

A third proposal was that, beyond the information provided in the national report, the Youth Directorate should identify its contacts within the host country and notify the international team; this would or could provide an additional strand to information-gathering.

44. It is important that, in the round, review team members are not left out of pocket. 'In the round' means that all legitimately receipted expenses for travel and subsistence costs incurred during a review are fully covered by the combination of per diem allowances and travel reimbursements. This is an absolutely minimum requirement.

45. A clearer sense of minimum 'requirements' – perhaps agreed by the whole team during a preliminary meeting – concerning attendance during the formal programme and during more social occasions would establish greater clarity for team members as to what is expected of them.

During each visit, based on team discussion and agreement, different team members should perhaps take the lead role in shaping and guiding the agenda within particular meetings during the formal programme.

At the conclusion of the second visit (or possibly at the very end of the process), the international review team should reflect on and evaluate how effectively it had worked as a team.

46. There was wholehearted support for the 'ideal' framework for the review process – the first visit to t he central administration, a period for exchange and consolidation, then a second visit to address emergent themes and more operational issues in the regions.

All reviews should involve at least two visits: even small countries have complex histories and challenging issues with which to grapple.

The shape and balance of the programme needs careful attention and considered negotiation between hosting groups and the international team (or its nominated lead).

In particular, space must be set aside, and defended, for the international team to be able to reflect on how its work is progressing and to plan properly for meetings that lie ahead.

47. There may be different reasons for maintaining contact between visits, but there is unlikely to be a good reason for not doing so at all. Simply sharing emergent information on the host country, stumbled upon by one individual or another, would be a 'bottom line'; a 'top line' would be the draft preparation by different team members of elements of the international report. Once more, the key point is that this should not be left to chance or in a vacuum, but purposefully debated.

48. If team members are to play a part in contributing to, or responding to, drafts of the international report, then this does need to be formalised in some way – possibly through some system of rewards or sanctions. Too often, material has been promised and never delivered. Too often, feedback has been requested, and never given. This places the rapporteur in an invidious position, especially where deadlines or hearings are looming.

Minority positions and perspectives within the international team obviously jeopardise the 'integrity' of the final international report, but there is now a model for accommodating them while retaining an overall consensual report.

New rapporteurs may benefit from having the opportunity to access advice, guidance and support from those who have previously fulfilled this role.

There is a strong case for the standardisation of international reports, using an agreed template (building on the existing synthesis report and adding quality standards concerning the process) and avoiding the duplication of material that should be in a national report.

49. It is imperative that the time allocations between different presenters at both the national and international hearings are fairly allocated and properly enforced, to ensure parity of opportunity and intervention.

50. Where commitments are made to following through issues raised in the international report, there should be a more formalised approach to reviewing and discussing subsequent policy development – perhaps after two years.

Appendix 2: A new framework for the international youth policy reviews

The nation in question – an overview

- Culture, history, politics and contemporary context

Conceptualising 'youth'

- Case studies, transitions and a 'youth sociology'

Conceptualising 'youth policy'

- Time scales, evolution, tradition and change

Delivery of youth policy

- Legislation and/or administrative arrangements
- Finance and budget; funding allocations
- Role of arm's-length national youth agency?
- Youth organisations and the government
- The National Youth Council
- Horizontal and vertical structures for delivery
- 'Delivery relationships' – policy to practice

Dimensions of youth policy

a. Policy domains

- Education
- Youth work and non-formal education
- Training and employment
- Health
- Social protection
- Values and religion
- Leisure and culture
- Military and alternative service
- Family policy and child welfare

- Housing
- Youth justice

b. *Cross-cutting issues*

- Youth participation and citizenship
- Social inclusion
- Youth information
- Multiculturalism and minorities
- Mobility and internationalism
- Equal opportunities
- Radicalisation and reaction
- Local v. global pressures
- The role of new technologies
- Centre–periphery relationships
- Urban–rural polarisation
- Elites and outsiders
- Environmental issues
- Diasporic influence

Foundation stones for effective youth policy

- Youth research
- Training of practitioners
- Dissemination of good practice

Benchmarks and indicators

Appendix 3: Guidelines for the implementation of national youth policy reviews

One of the priority objectives of intergovernmental co-operation in the youth field is to promote the development of youth policies in the member states, such as policies being understood as transversal policies, given that youth, by definition, is a multidisciplinary domain covering a wide range of society issues. Although the age range used for defining youth may differ from country to country, it should be underlined that, for the Council of Europe's youth policy, the main target group is constituted by young people aged between 15 and 25.

In 1997, as a means to implement this objective, the CDEJ incorporated the review of national youth policies into its intergovernmental programme. To date, seven countries have undergone a review (Finland, the Netherlands, Sweden, Spain, Romania, Estonia and Luxembourg). An eighth one is under way (Lithuania).

More recently, following a request from the Slovenian Government to the Directorate of Youth and Sport, a group of experts went to Slovenia from 21 to 24 May 2002 to provide advice on the preparation of draft legislation on youth policy to be submitted to the Slovenian Parliament, with the intention of reproducing this work format if it proved successful. In future, this new form of co-operation would concern countries which are not yet prepared to go through the process of national youth policy review but need advice or assistance in establishing or further developing their youth policy or some aspects of it.

Finally, also in the context of its youth policy development objectives, in 2003, the CDEJ will proceed to the elaboration of guidelines for the formulation and the implementation of youth policies, with a view to drafting a recommendation from the Committee of Ministers to the member states.

As far as the national youth policy reviews are concerned, the CDEJ and the partners concerned have regularly questioned themselves on the aims, methods and follow-up of this process, in particular as regards two important questions:

- How to ensure the national youth policy reviews are of real benefit to the country undergoing the review as well as to other countries?

- How to devise a process of analysis of the reviews allowing the development of youth policies based on shared principles, aims and content?

These concerns were at the centre of debates held during the consultative meeting on the evaluation of the programme of national youth policy reviews (16-17 December 2000). They were equally brought out in a detailed way in the synthesis report drawn up by Mr H. Williamson on the Council of Europe international reviews of national youth policies (1997-2001) "Supporting young people in Europe: principles, policy and practice".

The report by Mr Williamson discusses the strengths and weaknesses of the seven national youth reports and their international reviews; introduces a repertory of youth policy items as they appear in these reports; and highlights the sometimes-important differences in youth policy conceptualisation and practice. It also makes suggestions on how to achieve a higher level of comparability between the reviews. Finally, the report outlines the possible contents and methodology of a European approach to youth policy, based on some common principles, objectives and domains.

The time has now come to better define:

- the strategic place of these reviews within the overall priorities and objectives of the Directorate for Youth and Sport;

- how national youth reports are prepared;

- how to improve the methods used for presentation, discussion and follow-up of the reviews.

Guidelines for the implementation of national youth policy reviews

1. Objectives of the process of national youth policy reviews

The national youth policy reviews should have the following objectives:

a) to advise on key national youth policy issues as listed in paragraph 4.b;

b) to contribute to a learning process about the development and implementation of youth policy in Europe;

c) to identify components of youth policy which might inform an approach to 'youth policy' across Europe.

2. What are the necessary conditions for the implementation of the process

The basic conditions for the implementation of the national youth policy reviews are as follows:

a) respect of the specific national conditions and of the diversity of approaches to youth and youth policy in Europe;

b) consideration of the differences regarding the material and human resource based situations of youth research in member countries (reliability of data, inter-ministerial co-operation, training of staff in charge of research, level of development of civil society, etc.);

c) the acceptation, by the country concerned, of the above-mentioned objectives of the process;

d) agreement, with the member states volunteering for a report, on the main dimensions to be covered by the report, notably as a matter of comparability (actual size and content, translation into official languages of the Council of Europe, etc.);

e) the establishment of a co-ordinated approach regarding the international review process.

3. Implementation of the process

The national youth policy review process should be implemented in the following manner:

a) presentation of applications (roughly one year before starting to work on the national report);

b) inclusion in the intergovernmental programme of activities;

c) establishment of the international team of experts (one CDEJ member, one Advisory Council member and up to three experts, including at least one youth policy specialist and one researcher). One of the three last experts should be appointed rapporteur;

d) discussion between the country concerned and the rapporteur and/or other members of the international team on the detailed table of contents of the national report and the method of the analysis;

e) elaboration of the national report;

f) visits of the international team (two visits per country);

g) preparation of the international review, using a similar table of contents as the national report (other issues can be added if needed);

h) presentation of the international review in the country concerned, with public debate;

i) presentation of a summary report of the review and debate within the Joint Council, with the participation of the authorities of the country concerned (who will be invited to make comments on the process); examination of the recommendations from the international team and evaluation of the process (including decision on how to further improve it);

j) monitoring of the process, including:

- the preparation, after two years, of a brief report, by the country concerned, on developments which took place since the review and on the implementation of the recommendations stemming from the international report;

- if needed, the examination of complementary requests formulated by the country (expert visits, assistance, etc.);

- the elaboration, on a regular basis, of a synthesis report on the overall process (every four years).

4. What dimensions of youth policy should be covered by the national reports and international reviews?

The national reports should concentrate mainly on domains that concern youth and youth policy. Other domains of a general character (economic, social, political, demographical, etc.) should serve to better understand the "youth domain" and be reduced to the minimum (eventually, be appended). In this respect, national reports should in principle cover the dimensions listed under a. and b. below. The international reviews should mainly concentrate and give comments/opinions on key issues listed under b.:

a. Domains of youth policy

- education and training
- youth employment
- health related issues
- housing
- social protection
- family policy and child protection
- leisure, lifestyle and youth culture
- cultural policy
- juvenile justice and policy on delinquency prevention
- military and/or civil service, if any
- gender equality
- youth research

b. Key issues

- youth legislation and finance
- transversal dimension of youth policy
- transition from childhood to adulthood
- structures and networks for youth policy delivery, including youth research and youth information, as well as level of decentralisation
- participation and citizenship at local, regional and national levels
- fight against social exclusion and promotion of inclusion
- drug prevention
- multiculturalism and minorities
- handicapped youth
- youth work and non-formal education/learning
- mobility and voluntary service
- support to creativity and entrepreneurship
- youth participation in local and regional development
- equal opportunities
- security (violence in particular)

These indicative lists should be adapted to the specific characteristics of the country concerned (see point 3 above).

5. Outlook

The international reviews will take into account developments related to the White Paper on Youth of the European Commission and follow-up action taken on this.

When preparing the national reports and international reviews, some key items of the international youth policy debate should also be considered, such as globalisation, risk society, individualisation and consumption.

The results of the work of the group of specialists working on youth policy indicators shall be introduced into the review process once they have been produced and approved.

Bibliography

Arnett, J. (2004), *Emerging Adulthood: The Winding Road from Late Teens through the Twenties*, Oxford: Oxford University Press

Bynner, J. (2005), "Rethinking the Youth Phase of the Life-course: The Case for Emerging Adulthood?", *Journal of Youth Studies* Vol. 8 No. 4 pp. 367-84

Evans, K. (2005), "Foreword", in S. Warner Weil, D. Windemeersch and T. Jansen, *Unemployed Youth and Social Exclusion in Europe: Learning for Inclusion?*, Aldershot: Ashgate

Levitas, R. (2005), *The Inclusive Society? Social Exclusion and New Labour*, second edition, London: Palgrave

Rutter, M. and Smith, D. (eds) (1995), *Psychosocial Disorders in Young People: Time Trends and Their Causes*, Chichester: Wiley

Walther, A. and Stauber, B. (eds) (2002), *Misleading Trajectories*, EGRIS report, Opladen: Leske und Budrich

Williamson, H. and Hoskins, B. with Boetzelen, P. (eds) (2005), *Charting the Landscape of European Youth Voluntary Activities*, Strasbourg: Council of Europe Publishing

Sales agents for publications of the Council of Europe
Agents de vente des publications du Conseil de l'Europe

BELGIUM/BELGIQUE
La Librairie Européenne -
The European Bookshop
Rue de l'Orme, 1
B-1040 BRUXELLES
Tel.: +32 (0)2 231 04 35
Fax: +32 (0)2 735 08 60
E-mail: order@libeurop.be
http://www.libeurop.be

Jean De Lannoy
Avenue du Roi 202 Koningslaan
B-1190 BRUXELLES
Tel.: +32 (0)2 538 43 08
Fax: +32 (0)2 538 08 41
E-mail: jean.de.lannoy@dl-servi.com
http://www.jean-de-lannoy.be

CANADA
Renouf Publishing Co. Ltd.
1-5369 Canotek Road
OTTAWA, Ontario K1J 9J3, Canada
Tel.: +1 613 745 2665
Fax: +1 613 745 7660
Toll-Free Tel.: (866) 767-6766
E-mail: order.dept@renoufbooks.com
http://www.renoufbooks.com

CZECH REPUBLIC/
RÉPUBLIQUE TCHÈQUE
Suweco CZ, s.r.o.
Klecakova 347
CZ-180 21 PRAHA 9
Tel.: +420 2 424 59 204
Fax: +420 2 848 21 646
E-mail: import@suweco.cz
http://www.suweco.cz

DENMARK/DANEMARK
GAD
Vimmelskaftet 32
DK-1161 KØBENHAVN K
Tel.: +45 77 66 60 00
Fax: +45 77 66 60 01
E-mail: gad@gad.dk
http://www.gad.dk

FINLAND/FINLANDE
Akateeminen Kirjakauppa
PO Box 128
Keskuskatu 1
FIN-00100 HELSINKI
Tel.: +358 (0)9 121 4430
Fax: +358 (0)9 121 4242
E-mail: akatilaus@akateeminen.com
http://www.akateeminen.com

FRANCE
La Documentation française
(diffusion/distribution France entière)
124, rue Henri Barbusse
F-93308 AUBERVILLIERS CEDEX
Tél.: +33 (0)1 40 15 70 00
Fax: +33 (0)1 40 15 68 00
E-mail: commande@ladocumentationfrancaise.fr
http://www.ladocumentationfrancaise.fr

Librairie Kléber
1 rue des Francs Bourgeois
F-67000 STRASBOURG
Tel.: +33 (0)3 88 15 78 88
Fax: +33 (0)3 88 15 78 80
E-mail: francois.wolfermann@librairie-kleber.fr
http://www.librairie-kleber.com

GERMANY/ALLEMAGNE
AUSTRIA/AUTRICHE
UNO Verlag GmbH
August-Bebel-Allee 6
D-53175 BONN
Tel.: +49 (0)228 94 90 20
Fax: +49 (0)228 94 90 222
E-mail: bestellung@uno-verlag.de
http://www.uno-verlag.de

GREECE/GRÈCE
Librairie Kauffmann s.a.
Stadiou 28
GR-105 64 ATHINAI
Tel.: +30 210 32 55 321
Fax.: +30 210 32 30 320
E-mail: ord@otenet.gr
http://www.kauffmann.gr

HUNGARY/HONGRIE
Euro Info Service kft.
1137 Bp. Szent István krt. 12.
H-1137 BUDAPEST
Tel.: +36 (06)1 329 2170
Fax: +36 (06)1 349 2053
E-mail: euroinfo@euroinfo.hu
http://www.euroinfo.hu

ITALY/ITALIE
Licosa SpA
Via Duca di Calabria, 1/1
I-50125 FIRENZE
Tel.: +39 0556 483215
Fax: +39 0556 41257
E-mail: licosa@licosa.com
http://www.licosa.com

MEXICO/MEXIQUE
Mundi-Prensa México, S.A. De C.V.
Río Pánuco, 141 Delegacíon Cuauhtémoc
06500 MÉXICO, D.F.
Tel.: +52 (01)55 55 33 56 58
Fax: +52 (01)55 55 14 67 99
E-mail: mundiprensa@mundiprensa.com.mx
http://www.mundiprensa.com.mx

NETHERLANDS/PAYS-BAS
De Lindeboom Internationale Publicaties b.v.
M.A. de Ruyterstraat 20 A
NL-7482 BZ HAAKSBERGEN
Tel.: +31 (0)53 5740004
Fax: +31 (0)53 5729296
E-mail: books@delindeboom.com
http://www.delindeboom.com

NORWAY/NORVÈGE
Akademika
Postboks 84 Blindern
N-0314 OSLO
Tel.: +47 2 218 8100
Fax: +47 2 218 8103
E-mail: support@akademika.no
http://www.akademika.no

POLAND/POLOGNE
Ars Polona JSC
25 Obroncow Street
PL-03-933 WARSZAWA
Tel.: +48 (0)22 509 86 00
Fax: +48 (0)22 509 86 10
E-mail: arspolona@arspolona.com.pl
http://www.arspolona.com.pl

PORTUGAL
Livraria Portugal
(Dias & Andrade, Lda.)
Rua do Carmo, 70
P-1200-094 LISBOA
Tel.: +351 21 347 42 82 / 85
Fax: +351 21 347 02 64
E-mail: info@livrariaportugal.pt
http://www.livrariaportugal.pt

RUSSIAN FEDERATION/
FÉDÉRATION DE RUSSIE
Ves Mir
9a, Kolpacnhyi per.
RU-101000 MOSCOW
Tel.: +7 (8)495 623 6839
Fax: +7 (8)495 625 4269
E-mail: orders@vesmirbooks.ru
http://www.vesmirbooks.ru

SPAIN/ESPAGNE
Mundi-Prensa Libros, s.a.
Castelló, 37
E-28001 MADRID
Tel.: +34 914 36 37 00
Fax: +34 915 75 39 98
E-mail: libreria@mundiprensa.es
http://www.mundiprensa.com

SWITZERLAND/SUISSE
Van Diermen Editions – ADECO
Chemin du Lacuez 41
CH-1807 BLONAY
Tel.: +41 (0)21 943 26 73
Fax: +41 (0)21 943 36 05
E-mail: info@adeco.org
http://www.adeco.org

UNITED KINGDOM/ROYAUME-UNI
The Stationery Office Ltd
PO Box 29
GB-NORWICH NR3 1GN
Tel.: +44 (0)870 600 5522
Fax: +44 (0)870 600 5533
E-mail: book.enquiries@tso.co.uk
http://www.tsoshop.co.uk

UNITED STATES and CANADA/
ÉTATS-UNIS et CANADA
Manhattan Publishing Company
468 Albany Post Road
CROTTON-ON-HUDSON, NY 10520, USA
Tel.: +1 914 271 5194
Fax: +1 914 271 5856
E-mail: Info@manhattanpublishing.com
http://www.manhattanpublishing.com

Council of Europe Publishing/Editions du Conseil de l'Europe
F-67075 Strasbourg Cedex
Tel.: +33 (0)3 88 41 25 81 – Fax: +33 (0)3 88 41 39 10 – E-mail: publishing@coe.int – Website: http://book.coe.int